A MARRIAGE MANUAL

A Marriage Manual

Perry H. Biddle, Jr.

William B. Eerdmans Publishing Company
Grand Rapids, Michigan

First published 1974, 1987 by Abingdon Press, Nashville, Tennessee

Wm. B. Eerdmans Publishing Co.
255 Jefferson Ave. S.E., Grand Rapids, Michigan 49503

Printed in the United States of America

00 7 6 5 4 3

Library of Congress Cataloging-in-Publication Data

Biddle, Perry H., 1932-
A marriage manual / Perry H. Biddle, Jr. — Updated and rev. ed.
p. cm.
Rev. ed. of: Abingdon marriage manual. © 1987.
Includes bibliographical references.
ISBN 0-8028-0699-6
1. Marriage service. I. Biddle, Perry H., 1932-
Abingdon marriage manual. II. Title.
BV199.M3B52 1994
265′.5 — dc20 94-10970
CIP

For Sue,
who for more than thirty-five years
has been my soulmate, friend, wife,
and whose growing love continues
to enrich life

OTHER PUBLICATIONS BY THE AUTHOR

Abingdon Funeral Manual (1976; revised 1984)
Abingdon Marriage Manual (1974; revised 1986)
Abingdon Hospital Visitation Manual (1988)
A Funeral Manual (1994)
A Hospital Visitation Manual (1994)
Humor and Healing (1994)
Lectionary Preaching Workbook, Year B (1987)
Lectionary Preaching Workbook, Year C (1988)
Marrying Again (1986)
Preaching the Lectionary, Year A (1989)
Preaching the Lectionary, Year B (1990)
Preaching the Lectionary, Year C (1991)
Reflections on Suicide (1992)
The Goodness of Marriage (1984)

CONTENTS

PREFACE TO THE REISSUE

Rarely does an author have the opportunity to revise a book not once but twice. The earlier *Abingdon Marriage Manual* (1974; revised 1986) went through many printings before going out of print in 1992. I was delighted when Wm. B. Eerdmans Publishing Company offered a contract to reissue in a revised and updated form the widely used marriage manual.

This edition contains the newest liturgies available from a variety of denominations, including the new Presbyterian marriage service.

The section on music has been revised and newer music from the 1990s added. Hal Hopson, who suggested appropriate music for the original edition and revision, has also suggested music for this reissue. His compositions are especially recommended. I am grateful to church organists Edgar Rogers of Second Presbyterian Church, Nashville, and Andrew Risinger of First Presbyterian Church, Nashville, for reviewing the music sections and making helpful suggestions.

The former sample policy statement has been replaced with a revision dated March 1992 from Westminster Presbyterian Church, Nashville. I am grateful to its senior minister, Rev. K. C. Ptomey, and to the church for permission to include their excellent model wedding policy statement.

The bibliography of suggested resources contains some of the best books on preparing for marriage and working through issues in the first year of marriage, a strong emphasis of this manual.

I am grateful to Rev. Hoyt Hickman, former director of worship resources, Board of Discipleship of the United Methodist Church, and to the new director, Rev. Dan Benedict, for their help in preparing this revision. Others who have read the earlier book and made suggestions are Rev. Donna Scott, Rev. John Wilkerson, and Professor Robert Ramey.

Finally, I thank my wife of more than thirty-five years, Sue, for her encouragement in preparing this revision.

Nashville, Tennessee
September 1, 1993

PERRY H. BIDDLE, JR.

PREFACE TO THE REVISED EDITION

I have been deeply gratified by the favorable response to the first edition of this book. When *Christian Ministry* magazine, in its May 1986 issue, called it "*the* standard resource for pastors planning wedding ceremonies," I was extremely pleased. Many new ministers reported that as they left seminary they bought a copy and found it useful in conducting their first and subsequent weddings.

I am grateful to all those who helped make the first edition possible; to them goes much of the credit for the widespread use of the book.

We are living in an exciting time of liturgical development! A number of denominations have prepared new marriage rites. A carefully selected group of these new liturgies have been included in this revision, along with new approaches to the marriage ceremony and to ministry with couples.

I would like to express appreciation to several persons who have given valuable aid in bringing the book up to date. To Hoyt Hickman, retired director of worship resources of The General Board of Discipleship of The United Methodist Church, I give special thanks. Hal H. Hopson, former president of Westminster Choir College and one of the foremost composers of church music today, made valuable suggestions. I also wish to thank Rev. K. C.

Ptomey, minister at Westminster Presbyterian Church, Nashville, Tennessee, for permission to use "The Christian Service of Marriage," which contains guidelines for weddings and other helpful information. My good friend and colleague in ministry, Robert H. Crumby, minister emeritus of Donelson Presbyterian Church, has read the revisions and given suggestions.

Many clergy have given input over the thirteen years since the first edition appeared. I would be remiss not to mention members of the Academy of Parish Clergy, Inc., who responded to my questionnaire at the 1986 convocation, and the clergy who have participated in workshops I have led, all of whom have taught me much.

Finally, I want to express appreciation to my wife of twenty-eight years, Sue, who does not type manuscripts, but who encouraged me to buy a word processor, which assisted greatly in the revision of this book. She continues to make our marriage sparkle with joy and love.

Old Hickory, Tennessee PERRY H. BIDDLE, JR.
Advent 1986

PART I

ARRANGING THE WEDDING

1

PRESENT-DAY CONCERNS AND CELEBRATIONS

For more than twenty years I have had the opportunity to lead workshops for clergy on seminary campuses and in other settings. We examined the wedding ceremony and the pastoral care related to uniting couples in marriage, and in the informal give-and-take of such workshops I have learned much from my colleagues which I hope will be useful to other clergy. I have been particularly impressed by the intentional, responsible fashion in which many clergy perform their role — preparing couples for marriage, performing the ceremony, and following up in the subsequent months.

As part of the research for preparing this book I devised a brief survey sheet about wedding ceremonies and related issues which I circulated at the 1986 annual convocation of the Academy of Parish Clergy, Inc. The members who responded were from mainline Protestant and Roman Catholic churches across North America. No attempt will be made to offer the results as a scientific survey of current practices, but information from the survey will be shared in this and other chapters. For instance, recently there has been a movement toward more traditional weddings and a more conservative approach toward sexual matters and commitment in marriage.

During the years since I wrote the first edition I have talked informally with many clergy about their wedding service practices, have attended weddings as a guest, have continued to guide couples in planning their ceremonies, and have conducted those services. This revised edition, like the first, is written by a working pastor for working pastors, to enable them to become more effective in ministering to couples before and after the wedding ceremony and in conducting the ceremony itself. The following insights, experiences, and suggestions are offered in the hope that Christian marriage ceremonies may become more meaningful services of worship, in which a man and a woman covenant to live together for the rest of their lives.

The Marriage License

The minister wears two hats in performing a wedding ceremony. He or she serves as a minister of Jesus Christ in setting forth the church's understanding of marriage based in Scripture and tradition, hears the vows, and offers the church's blessing on the covenant made by the couple. But he or she *also represents the state.* It is the minister's duty to make sure the marriage license is valid and that it is filled out correctly and returned to the proper official, as required by law. Because the minister carries out this function of the state, the *marriage license must be in the minister's hands* ***before*** *a wedding ceremony is conducted.*

The minister should suggest to the couple that the license be obtained several days prior to the wedding and that it be brought to the wedding rehearsal, if not given to the minister earlier. The minister may guide the couple in what is required in obtaining a license — cost, place of purchase, and so on. The license is valid for thirty days or so and therefore should not be purchased too early, but neither should the couple wait until the last day.

One couple went to obtain their license on the Friday before their large formal Saturday-evening church wedding, only to find that because of snow and ice on the streets the license bureau had closed at 11:00 that morning. When their minister consulted a judge, he was told that there was no way to obtain a license before the following Monday. So the entire wedding party and those guests who could stay in town were forced to wait until Monday evening for the ceremony.

A minister in the Northeast reported performing a wedding ceremony without the wedding license, but with the groom's solemn promise that he would bring it the next day. Instead, the couple went to Hawaii for a ten-day honeymoon. The minister spent many sleepless nights, but when the couple returned, they brought the license to the minister, and it was then properly filed with the county clerk's office.

There is a new laxity abroad regarding laws, and this has carried over into laws governing marriage. While some clergy are "blessing relationships" that are not legally recognized, this is not a practice to be commended. If ministers take the law into their own hands and perform ceremonies without licenses, they not only may be embarrassed but may find their credibility with the congregation and community greatly diminished as a result. In researching this matter in Tennessee law, I have not discovered that a minister would be liable to fines or other punishment. However, one could be called before the church's governing body for whatever action it might take.

The minister is required by law to file the license within a certain period of time (three days, for example) with the county clerk's office. The minister should be very scrupulous about this, making sure that there is a stamp and a return address on the envelope and that the envelope is mailed. Or the minister may deliver the signed license in person. Many states impose a fine if the license is not returned in the required time period. This is one part of the minister's work in which Paul's admonition, "Let every person be subject to the governing authorities" (Rom. 13:1), should be heeded. If the minister loses the license or fails to return it for any reason, the couple may have difficulty obtaining an official copy of it later for legal or business purposes.

Planning for Harmonious Relationships

With the greatly increased rate of divorce in recent years, we can anticipate that one out of every two marriages may end in divorce. This means that many couples are from families in which the parents have been divorced at least once. In addition to blending two families that may meet for the first time at the wedding rehearsal, the wedding brings together ex-husbands and ex-wives. Planning the seating of those formerly married persons at the wedding and rehearsal dinner and their places in the reception line and at other related occasions can call forth the best wisdom of minister, wedding consultant, bride, and groom.

The minister should *plan ahead* with the couple as to who will be invited to the wedding, the rehearsal dinner, and so on, and their interaction with other persons. This can help prevent embarrassing situations, promote harmonious relationships, and prevent hurt feelings and angry outbursts that would dampen the joy of the occasion. A number of wedding etiquette books offer useful information on such matters.

Hostile feelings on the part of members of the wedding party could affect the bride and groom as they begin married life together. The minister, as spiritual leader, also should be sensitive to the gestalt of the two families. Counseling, formally or informally, with family members before, during, or after the celebrations that surround the wedding might be one of the best ways to help the new couple make a successful beginning. An alienated father, mother, or other relative may be led to work through negative feelings and become supportive of the couple; parents may be enabled emotionally to "turn loose" the child who has married. The need for this is pointed up by the mother who insisted that her daughter call home each night of her honeymoon!

Interfaith Weddings

When the minister is asked to participate in an interfaith (Jewish or Islamic) wedding, the minister should plan with the other clergy person so that the integrity of both faiths is maintained. This may mean that one clergy person reads a portion of Scripture or offers a prayer and the other leads the Christian or the Jewish or Islamic wedding service. Or the couple may choose to have two services, with each faith leader conducting one service alone. This is recommended as the only solution to an interreligious (Christian and other world religion) service. The Hindu or Shinto wedding service is conducted and then the

Christian wedding service is conducted. To attempt to amalgamate the two produces a service that compromises each religion and should be avoided. (For books on this subject, see the bibliography.)

Decorum in the Wedding Ceremony

The self-centeredness of recent years has put a strain on human relationships, especially in gatherings such as weddings. It sometimes appears that America has moved from barbarism to decadence without passing through civilization, as one British college debating team argued successfully against an American team a few years ago.

While the minister may view the wedding ceremony as a service of Christian worship, those without Christian training may see it as a spectacle, much like a circus or a rock concert, at which any kind of behavior goes. Loud talking, photographers, crying babies, beepers, alarm watches — all detract from the appropriate mood for a Christian service of worship. Commercial video-camera operators have even attempted to invade weddings to make a tape of the ceremony that they try to sell to the couple later!

The wise minister plans ahead to avoid being put in the position of being a "sergeant at arms" in attempting to maintain order. If a church's policy statement on weddings deals with decorum, this may be published in the wedding bulletin and, if necessary, brought to the attention of the congregation by the minister.

Some churches deal with photographers by instructing the ushers to ask guests to leave their cameras in the narthex until after the ceremony, when the wedding party will pose for pictures. The provision of a nursery will prevent crying babies from destroying the mood of the service; ushers may be instructed to ask parents of children under three years of age to take them to the nursery.

There are communities and cultures, however, where babies, crying or not, are considered such an important part of a ceremony that they are not only accepted but welcomed. The minister to a new community would do well to inquire about such practices before attempting to make radical changes.

Couples Already Living Together

An informal survey of clergy across the nation reveals that forty-one percent of the couples they united in marriage in 1985 were already living together. This varied, with one minister reporting all six couples living together, and another reporting none of the three he married doing so. One older minister indicated that in 1965 only ten percent of the couples were living together before the wedding, whereas twenty years later in 1985 fifty percent were doing so. Another reported none living together in 1965, but fifty percent in 1985.

When I served as an assistant minister in Scotland in 1958, the sessional records from a century or two earlier revealed that the usual procedure for marriage in such cases was as follows: The couple was brought before the church session when the woman was obviously pregnant. The couple would confess their sin of fornication and ask forgiveness and permission to be married in the church. This would be granted, and the couple was then married.

This historical account is related, not to justify the current practice, but to point out that it is not a recent development. Many clergy today feel as one minister does. When asked how the living-together phenomenon had made him feel about counseling such couples before marriage, he replied, "Cynical and frustrated."

Many ministers are finding it helpful to ask the couple in the first premarital interview where they are in their relationship. One minister routinely asks if the woman is pregnant in order to discover if there are unusual pressures on the couple to marry. Another says that if he doesn't already know whether the couple is living together (and he adds that he usually does know), this is one of the first questions he asks. Then he tries to explore, in a helpful, nonjudgmental way, their thoughts on the meaning of marriage. He asks, "Why be married? What difference does it make?" If the couple confesses what seems to be a sincere Christian faith and church involvement, he asks how they see living together in relation to the moral teachings of their church (or churches). Otherwise, his counseling is about the same as with other couples.

One minister says that she treats such couples the same as others but finds that they may think they are more prepared for marriage, which is generally not the case. Another minister indicates that he does not treat living together before marriage as an issue unless the couple raises it as such. And another says that if the couple is living together, this does change his approach to many areas of premarital counseling.

A minister of a large church indicates his opinion that couples already living together do have more realistic expectations of the practical aspects of cooperative living. He goes on to say, however, that he believes "living together before the wedding indicates less idealistic trust in each other. Many of these people themselves come from broken homes." A minister in a small town in a western state says that in counseling those already living together he uses a marriage enrichment program designed for couples married at least six months.

Ministers who follow up with these couples in the months following the wedding indicate that the commitment made in marriage changes their relationship dramatically. Although the partners may have "walked on eggshells" while living together to avoid hurting each other's feelings or arousing anger, once they are married a new dynamic begins. They may have kept their money in separate accounts, kept house or cars in separate names, and expressed their individuality and independence in other ways, but when they are married they go through the same "newlywed" dynamics as other couples. Therefore neither the minister nor the couple should assume that they are better prepared for marriage because of having lived together.

In fact, some counselors and ministers report a *negative* reaction in the early stages of marriage. One or both partners may feel guilt for having lived together. They may have "gunnysacked" their hurt feelings, anger, and resentment, but once they are married they may dump their sacks of past anger and create a crisis. Or one partner may have felt pressured into the marriage and may express resentment.

The minister who counsels couples living together should not assume that they know very much about human sexuality, beyond the physical aspects. Sexual intercourse before marriage (and sometimes after) often is a selfish using of each other. Premarital counseling should instruct couples in the meaning of Christian marriage and the Christian understanding of sex. Both men and women should be encouraged to read about male and female sexuality (see bibliography).

A radical approach to working with couples seeking to be married — both those living together and those not living together — has been developed by religious leaders in Modesto, California. The couples sign a covenant that requires a four-month minimum waiting period, during which time they must complete at least two premarital counseling sessions. This policy was formulated by the Greater Modesto Ministerial Association.[1]

The Reverend James Talley, minister for singles at the First Baptist Church in Modesto, led the ministerial association in requiring a waiting period and counseling. In a telephone conversation, he reported that in a former job as a quality-control engineer he had learned the importance of checking on the results of a process. With the fifty percent breakdown of marriages in America, Talley decided that it was time ministers joined together to correct the problem.

The church Talley serves insists on an eight-month waiting period. During the first four months, couples must agree not to engage in any physical touching — even hand-holding. A couple living together must find separate housing; the church will help if this is a financial problem. The man and woman may see each other only five hours a month. During the last four months, they must agree to eight sessions with a church instructor on marriage.

1. See *The Christian Century*, June 4-11, 1986.

Talley reports that half the couples who take the course decide not to marry. This counseling and waiting period, says Talley, is an effective divorce preventive.

Talley is the author of *Too Close Too Soon, Too Close Too Soon Workbook,* and *Reconcilable Differences.* He also leads seminars for divorced persons to help them become reconciled and remarry their previous partners.

While it is true that preparation for marriage takes place over a lifetime and is learned in one's family of origin and by observing other marriages, it is my conviction that the responsibility for more effective ministry to couples, both before and after the wedding, lies with the minister. Ministers should not assume that they have the capacity to fully prepare a couple for marriage in a few brief counseling sessions, nor should they feel responsible for doing so. But at the same time, excellent books, personality tests, and other materials are available to assist them in developing a systematic and thorough program for preparing youths and couples of all ages for marriage.

Renewal of Marriage Vows

Many couples find meaning in renewing their marriage vows on special occasions such as the fifth, tenth, twenty-fifth, or fiftieth anniversary. In addition, each wedding that a couple attends offers an opportunity to renew the marriage vows. According to the new *Christian Marriage Service,* Supplemental Liturgical Resource 3 of the Presbyterian Church (U.S.A.),

> it is important to note that the marriage liturgy serves not only the couple in their marriage but also all others who

> are present. The service provides opportunities for all to remember promises they have made and to recommit themselves to those promises. As vows are spoken, married couples can renew their own vows. The statements about marriage, the lessons from Scripture, and the prayers remind the congregation of their mission to all families and challenge the people to exercise their responsibilities for mutual support and care.

A statement in the wedding bulletin may remind couples that the wedding can be a time to renew their vows. The minister may want to mention this in the wedding homily or in the welcome to the congregation.

When a special service to renew wedding vows is celebrated, the words in the marriage ritual selected may be changed to indicate that it is a renewal of vows. Instead of "I take you for my wife (husband) . . ." the vow would be stated "I continue to take you. . . ." If the rings are used again, words such as *rededicate* or *renew* may be used, and the prayers and homily would reflect that the vows are being renewed.

Renewal of vows may take place at a couple's home in a family celebration, in a garden or park, or in church. Members of the family and friends may be involved in leading the service, offering prayers, or reading Scripture.

The couple may want to use the same wedding service that was used when they were first married, but with appropriate alteration of words as indicated above.

Developments in Ministry to Couples

While it is not within the scope of this book to give more than a brief overview of new developments in premarital counseling and marriage enrichment, there has been commendable advancement in this field. Some resources in particular give an indication of the changes that have taken place and the kinds of materials now available. (For these and other resources, see the bibliography.)

Preparing for Christian Marriage, Pastor's Manual by Antoinette and Leon Smith is the most complete, thorough, and useful book I have reviewed. It is written by two leading authorities on marriage and sexuality, a husband and wife team, and is biblically grounded while incorporating the best of insights from recent personality testing, psychology, and communication theory. This book is user-friendly and walks the pastor through each suggested premarital counseling session. Four interviews with the couple before the wedding and one afterward are recommended by the Smiths. The fifth interview should take place from one to six months after the wedding. More emphasis is being placed on ministry to couples *after* the wedding, a movement noted in the first edition of the *Abingdon Marriage Manual.*

The companion couples' manual, *Preparing for Christian Marriage* by Joan and Richard Hunt, deals with various aspects of marriage, including such issues as which jobs each partner will do to keep their residence livable. They suggest exchanging the jobs of cooking, washing dishes, repairs, and cleaning. One Canadian professor of marriage and family living has indicated that household jobs and decisions often are the center of major conflicts in marriage. A copy of this book should be given to each couple in the first interview; future interviews on expectations, communication, sexuality, change, family, and so on are based on chapters in the book.

Premarital Counseling Handbook for Ministers is written by Theodore K. Pitt, the senior minister of a Baptist church in Rhode Island. Pitt recommends eight sessions of counseling, during which the pastor involves the couple in exercises to develop communication skills, self-understanding, and problem-solving abilities.

Pitt describes group workshops for couples preparing for marriage. This is an approach that is being used more widely and is highly recommended. Couples learn from one another and from the older married couples who lead the group sessions. The author includes guidelines for couples wishing to develop their own marriage covenants and also deals with divorce and remarriage. This book should be a resource in every minister's library.

In the Prepare-Enrich series (see bibliography) two programs are available: "Prepare," for unmarried couples without children, and "Enrich," for married couples and all couples with children. The programs were developed by David H. Olson, David G. Fournier, and Joan M. Druckman. Dr. Olson is an experiment station scientist in the Department of Family Social Science at the University of Minnesota.

Both programs consist of inventories that contain 115 items that will be used to encourage and enhance couple communication by identifying "relationship strengths" and "work areas." The couple meets with a minister or counselor, and each rates these items on a five-point scale. There are no right or wrong answers. When the inventories are computer scored, couples learn what they have in common that they can build on and where they need help. They then meet with the minister to talk over their relationship strengths and work areas, and they are encouraged to begin immediately to resolve items in their work areas.

The program generates discussion, since couples tend to be more honest on a questionnaire than when face to face. The "Prepare" program should be used in conjunction with the program of premarriage ministry that the minister chooses and develops for the congregation he or she serves. Olson recommends that after six months or a year the couple should return to use the "Enrich" program. More than one thousand clergy in Minnesota have used these programs, and many require their use.

The survey of Academy of Parish Clergy members reveals that the clergy who responded require an average of three sessions of sixty minutes each with couples preparing for marriage. Several require four sessions, and a few require ninety-minute sessions.

SECOND OR SUBSEQUENT MARRIAGES

The average divorce rate in the United States is near fifty percent. Combined with this, the death of spouses at various ages means that a large number of persons seeking to be married have been married previously.

My book *Marrying Again* was prepared to assist couples and the minister in planning for the second (or subsequent) marriage. The key to making a second marriage work is *realized forgiveness* for the mistakes, hurts, and errors of the previous marriage.

Couples marrying again usually are more serious about wanting premarital counseling; they understand more clearly the issues involved. The second wedding ceremony is often a small family affair when the bride has been married before. If she has not, the wedding usually is more elaborate.

Devotional Books for Newlyweds

There is a growing interest in the spiritual development of couples beginning married life. Many clergy are giving a copy of a devotional book to each couple as a wedding gift, inscribed with the date and place of the ceremony and a personal note of good wishes. While in the past some books of this nature were overly sentimental and failed to deal with the negative as well as the positive aspects of marriage, recent books are better balanced and more biblical in approach.

In the Presence of God by David and Vera Mace is a revision of a classic in the field, *Whom God Hath Joined.* The book leads the couple through the first weeks of marriage with a devotional for each day and inspirational reflections on various aspects of marriage. Vera Mace and her late husband, David, are world renowned in the field of marriage enrichment.

My volume *The Goodness of Marriage* is a gift book of meditations for the first four weeks of marriage. The meditations cover topics such as forgiveness, communication, sex, money, and family, and each concludes with a brief prayer. Couples of all ages, as well as young newlyweds, will find it helpful in developing a shared spiritual life.

2

MINISTRY BEFORE AND AFTER THE CEREMONY

The church and its clergy have a unique opportunity to prepare persons for marriage and to offer a follow-up ministry in the months and years after the wedding. The proclamation of the biblical message of God's judgment and grace and the administration of the sacraments are channels of God's gracious mercy to individuals and to couples. In the fellowship of believers, forgiveness and love are received and given. There a new quality of life is experienced. The concern of the people of God for others can be expressed in a very significant way through a ministry to persons before and after the wedding ceremony.

Many forces are at work to shape the lives of those preparing for marriage. Some are positive; others are negative. Family life is one of the more important of these forces. Christian family life is the *most* important. In the family where Christ is central, persons learn how to live, love, and function as husband and wife from the example of their parents.

Economic, social, and political as well as religious forces in society affect persons' preparation for marriage. For example, the liberation of women (especially economic) has radically changed traditional roles in marriage and society. A woman no longer seeks marriage or needs to remain married in order to find security and to be accepted in society.

The wise pastor will become more aware of these forces at work shaping the lives of old and young alike as they prepare for marriage or live as husband and wife. The pastor will recognize the limitations and strengths of the ministry the church can offer. Through participation in continuing theological education and other educational opportunities, the concerned pastor will seek to keep abreast of developments in pastoral ministry, especially as they relate to marriage and the family.

Ministry Before the Wedding Ceremony

In recent years great emphasis has been placed on the importance of premarital counseling. It has been advocated as a means of launching couples onto the sea of wedded bliss with greater odds for happiness. It has been taught as a means of reducing the rising divorce rate, creating a more stable family life, and insuring the future of the monogamous marriage. Many couples expect premarital counseling. Even most secular wedding planning guides mention premarital counseling by the pastor as an item not to be overlooked in planning for the wedding, since it can take advantage of a "teachable moment."

Every minister who joins a couple engages in some form of ministry to them before and after the ceremony. The crucial question is, what kind?

There is growing dissatisfaction on the part of some pastors and other professionals with traditional premarital counseling. Ministry *after* the ceremony is being stressed more now than in the past. One professor of pastoral counseling says that most couples, unless they come at their own initiative and seek specific help, are not receptive to the kind of premarital counseling that most ministers seem duty-bound to provide.

Another professor of pastoral counseling is even more pessimistic. He says that by the time the young couple comes to the minister, they seem impervious to anything that may be said or done, although they will agree to practically any proposal the minister makes.

During courtship, individuals lose most of their judgment. By definition, persons "in love" are in such a dizzy state that they become reckless. The problems of marriage are not noticed or considered. Occasionally the bride and groom know they are marrying the wrong person, but they are in such a passion and are being driven so hard by the applause of society that they feel they cannot help themselves.

One weepy young bride hysterically insisted on backing out of the wedding three minutes before the ceremony began. But the caterer persuaded her to go through with it! If this is the case, what ministry, if any, can a concerned pastor have to couples preparing for marriage?

Often there is another subtle but very real obstacle to premarital counseling: the opposing assumptions held by the couple and the pastor. The engaged couple asks their minister to marry them because they have finally reached a common decision that they are ready to be married. But the minister, guided by much of the current literature on premarital counseling, may assume that there is something "wrong" with the personality factors of the man or woman, and some "static" is assumed to exist in their communication with each other which needs to be eliminated. The literature challenges the minister to uncover these difficulties and, through the proper premarital counseling technique, to heal them and their relationship before marrying them. But unless the couple can be persuaded to set aside their assumptions and adopt the minister's, counseling cannot take place. And to attempt to so persuade them is to play God!

Couples may shy away from premarital counseling because of the negative connotations of "counseling" and the fear of invasion of privacy. "Preparation for marriage ministry" is a better term, and its use should be encouraged.

A good rule of thumb to follow in conducting such interviews is this: *Don't assume anything!* The pastor should attempt to create an open, trusting, supportive relationship that will continue after the wedding. In fact, some ministers feel that this may be the most valuable aspect of such interviews. And through posing the right questions, the minister can gain greater knowledge about the couple and about the ways in which the church can minister to them both now and later.

For example, unless you know the couple well, do *not* assume that neither has not been married and divorced. And it should never be assumed that they hold to traditional values and attitudes about marriage and premarital chastity.

Knowledge of previous marriages or of an already existing intimate relationship will allow the minister to provide a more appropriate ministry. Careful, sensitive listening by the minister will provide clues. This can be done without prying, probing, or invading privacy — much as a physician follows up clues to an illness in order to offer healing.

Each minister inevitably develops his or her own style of ministry for preparing couples for marriage. The alert, creative, caring pastor will continue to reshape this ministry. While a program of interviews, books, and tests may evolve, the pastor will be ever seeking to improve the ministry offered.

Three possible goals for the initial premarriage interview are these:

1. Determine whether the minister can, in good conscience and according to the rules of discipline of the denomination, participate in this event.
2. Offer a series of two or three additional conferences in order to *(a)* assist the couple in clarifying the terms of their marriage contract; *(b)* review the meaning of Christian marriage, particularly the vows; and *(c)* discuss the rehearsal and ceremony itself.
3. Set up a series of conferences after the ceremony — with the couple alone or with other couples — for "on the job training" in marriage.

During the initial interview the minister should be able to determine how many additional conferences will be desired before the wedding. But this question may be left somewhat open. If the minister can in good conscience marry the couple, the schedule will be checked to make certain the dates for both rehearsal and wedding are open; these dates will be cleared with the church office, organist, custodian, and other personnel. The pastor will also have discovered whether both are of legal age to be married without parental consent. If they are not, the pastor will ask for conferences with any parent(s) who objects to the marriage. Even when the couple is of legal age, it is advisable to have a conference with any parent(s) who does not favor the marriage.

If either party has been married previously, the pastor will be especially sensitive to any needs that may be expressed. Individual counseling may be offered in order to enable that person to work through any still-existing negative feelings that might affect the new marriage. James G. Emerson, in *Divorce, the Church and Remarriage,* sets forth his criterion of "realized forgiveness" in regard to the remarriage of divorced persons.[1] The pastor counseling persons who are divorced and preparing for remarriage will find this a very helpful resource. Should either party be divorced, the minister may want to consult with an advisory committee appointed for this purpose by his or her church's governing board or judicatory.

If the couple accepts the pastor's offer to meet with them for additional interviews in preparation for marriage, they should schedule the next meeting before concluding the first interview. These conferences will be aimed primarily at helping the couple clarify the terms of their marriage contract and gain a better grasp of the meaning of Christian marriage.

Charles William Stewart, in *The Minister as Marriage Counselor: Revised,* outlines the following marriage preparation interviews:

1. Emerson, *Divorce, the Church and Remarriage* (Philadelphia: Westminster Press, 1961), p. 23.

Interview One

The minister sees each partner separately to discuss their romance, their common interests, their relationships to both families, their understanding of sex, and the planning of family. . . .

Interview Two

The minister sees the couple together to discuss their budget, their planning of a home, and the values by which they live. He asks them to bring in a sample budget as a basis of discussion for this session.

Interview Three

The minister sees the couple together to discuss their interests, how they resolve conflicts, and their adjustment to difficulties. The latter part of the interview is used to discuss the religious side of marriage with the marriage ritual as the focus of discussion.[2]

The author, a recognized authority on marriage counseling, advocates flexibility in the use of this proposed schedule. The pastor should allow for individual differences among partners and for the uniqueness of each relationship.

A significant recent development in the ministry of preparing couples for marriage is *group seminars.* One

2. Stewart, *The Minister as Marriage Counselor: Revised* (Nashville: Abingdon Press, 1970), p. 61.

such program was offered on a university campus by a University Common Ministry composed of six denominations, including Roman Catholic. A modest fee was charged each couple to cover costs of materials and honoraria for speakers. The major areas of concern in marriage were presented by speakers or films and then discussed in small groups led by clergy. The two-hour seminars were offered on six successive Sunday evenings. A similar program could be offered by a church or by a group of churches each year, or more often.

In support of this approach, one authority says that *group* counseling is one of the most promising movements to help young people prepare more adequately for marriage. A professor of pastoral counseling affirms that a great deal can be accomplished in group counseling that cannot be accomplished with couples alone. He writes that, ideally, the church should make both experiences available. Lyle B. Gangsei's *Manual for Group Premarital Counseling* (New York: Association Press, 1971) offers concrete suggestions for planning such a ministry. Other helpful materials will be found in the annotated bibliography at the end of this manual. One such book resource is a classic on sex in marriage entitled *Intended for Pleasure* by husband and wife authors Ed Wheat, M.D., and Gaye Wheat (see bibliography). Their book is a complete sex manual with basic information, illustrations, and frank discussion of all phases of human sexuality. It has been revised and updated. The book can be useful for pastors and counselors working with couples as well as for couples themselves.

Clergy seeking to strengthen ministry to couples preparing for marriage would do well to read selectively in the literature currently available and then to shape a program that corresponds to his or her abilities, interests, and time available and the needs of those who come to be married. While recognizing the limitations and opportunities in this area, the caring pastor can continue to offer a supportive and educative ministry to those willing to accept it.

Ministry after the Wedding Ceremony

The ministry of the pastor and the church before and after the wedding are not two separate ministries but simply two phases of a single ministry. The *follow-up ministry*, rather than premarital counseling, is now being recognized by many pastors and other professionals as the more crucial of the two.

A well-known professor of pastoral care says that, while he thinks postmarital counseling is more critical than premarital, he does not think this eliminates the necessity for premarital counseling. After the wedding ceremony the couple is more open, and a great deal can be accomplished in the weeks that follow. This fairly recent emphasis recognizes the crucial nature of the first few months, when the terms of the marriage contract are being negotiated and husband and wife roles are being shaped.

Two classical writers on this subject, Fishbein and Burgess, claim that most marriages are made permanent or are lost in the first two or three months.[3] Recognizing the crucial importance of those early months, Howard Hovde has written *The Neo-Married* to assist in providing an effective ministry to couples recently married. Hovde points out

3. Morris Fishbein and Ernest W. Burgess, eds., *Successful Marriage* (Garden City, NY: Doubleday, 1951), p. 139.

that, although the third year of marriage is often considered the hardest because most divorces occur at that point, the time involved in deciding to divorce and going through the procedures indicates that the primary trouble year is the first. It is during the *early months of their married life* that couples develop the *patterns of behavior* they will follow later. How successful they are in this early period will greatly affect the rest of their marriage.[4]

Tom McGinnis, in *Your First Year of Marriage,* agrees that the first year of marriage is the crucial one. During this time individual and marital patterns of feeling, thinking, and acting are developed which tend to persist. These patterns, says McGinnis, determine to a large extent how happy and successful one's marriage will be. One of America's foremost marriage counselors, McGinnis says that the first year of marriage may well be the most exciting and challenging year of a person's life.[5]

For too long pastors have emphasized premarital counseling but neglected ministry to couples *after* the wedding ceremony. Having pronounced them man and wife and signed the wedding certificate, the pastor often allows them to fade into the church's woodwork to struggle alone through the crucial and formative first months of marriage. The pastor may drop by for a social visit or call to recruit the husband or wife for church membership or participation in the young adult church school class, but no true *ministry* will be offered.

4. Hovde, *The Neo-Married* (Valley Forge, PA: Judson Press, 1968), p. 13.

5. McGinnis, *Your First Year of Marriage* (Garden City, NY: Doubleday, 1967), pp. 1-8.

The minister of one of America's best-known pulpits reveals what is probably true in most churches today. "I have no particular strategy for post-wedding counseling," he writes. "If the couple is a part of the life of the parish one is serving, one will be able to stay in touch." But more than "staying in touch" is needed to enable couples to develop growing, vital, satisfactory marriage relationships. A creative, vigorous, continuing ministry by clergy and church is called for if the challenge is to be met.

There are many excellent resources to enable the pastor and congregation to develop a supportive ministry to newlyweds. Out of print but possibly available in libraries, a series of cassette tapes with printed guides, *Growth Counseling: New Tools for Clergy and Laity* by Howard J. and Charlotte H. Clinebell, is one of the best refresher courses for clergy.[6] The subjects most helpful in providing ministry to the married are these: "Leading a Marriage Growth Group"; "Highlights of a Marriage Enrichment Workshop"; "Using Marriage Problems for Growth"; and "Enhancing Sexual Intimacy in Marriage."

If the pastor elects to have a series of conferences with the couple alone rather than a group seminar, there will be greater flexibility in shaping the conferences to meet the particular needs of the couple. Two books mentioned earlier, *The Neo-Married* and *Your First Year of Marriage,* are excellent resources for structuring a series of marriage conferences with a couple. The newlyweds might be asked to read one or both books. Another book that commends

6. Clinebell and Clinebell, *Growth Counseling: New Tools for Clergy and Laity* (Nashville: Abingdon Press, 1973).

itself for use in post- or prewedding ministry is David R. Mace's *Getting Ready for Marriage: Revised,* designed for couples who may not have access to formal counseling by a professional (see bibliography). It would be an excellent book to put into the hands of a couple unable to meet for postwedding conferences.

Several group-oriented programs can be adapted for postwedding ministry. All are biblically sound and make use of the best insights from the human sciences. A request for further information and names of representatives in your area will enable a pastor and governing board to consider any or all of these programs:

1. National Presbyterian Mariners, 8353 W. 70th Place, Arvada, CO 80002
2. Association of Couples for Marriage Enrichment (ACME), P.O. Box 10596, Winston-Salem, NC 27108. Ph. (919) 724-1526
3. Your denomination's Family Ministry Department.

One local church formed a group for newlyweds called "The Ring and the Book," from the poem by Robert Browning. The group sought to combine the values of marriage and faith. While it had the usual social dimensions — suppers, outings, and so on — it also included intimate sharing of selves; expectations of mates, marriage, and life; book reviews; and studies in the field of personal relationships and family life. Occasionally the group went on a weekend retreat.

Two books especially suited for use in such a group are *Meet Me in the Middle* by Charlotte H. Clinebell (see bibliography) and *Till Divorce Do Us Part* by Lofton Hudson

(Nashville: T. Nelson, 1973). The first, written in light of the women's liberation movement, asserts that it is the woman who must take the initiative in changing the balance within the marriage relationship. It is a radical application of freedom to the dilemma of the modern woman. Hudson's book gives valuable help in building healthy, open, growing marriage relationships.

Some limitation may need to be placed on membership in such groups if they are to serve their purpose. One group agreed that a couple graduated from the group when their first child arrived. Some limit membership to couples married five years or less. Others limit the combined ages of the couple.

Programs for such groups usually revolve around the major concerns of marriage. Often local doctors, bankers, investors, ministers, and marriage counselors are asked to speak and lead discussions on a topic. Or programs may be led by members of the group.

A newlywed group might form a book discussion fellowship and supper club coordinated by a pastor or a couple. A different couple each time could give a book review and the group join in discussing the issue raised.

Vera Mace and her late husband, David, founders of the Association of Couples for Marriage Enrichment (ACME) and authorities on marriage, have suggested a six-week program, using their book *How to Have a Happy Marriage.* A group of couples could work through the book together, meeting each week to report on their progress. The Maces list three essentials for success in marriage: "(1) A commitment to growth, sincerely entered into by husband and wife together; (2) An effective communication system and the necessary skills to use it; (3) The ability to accept marital conflict positively and to resolve it creatively."[7]

The main headings in the book are "A Growth Plan for Your Marriage," "An Honest Look at Your Relationship," "Learning to Communicate Effectively," "Resolving Conflicts Creatively," and "Where Do We Go From Here?" The Maces point out that one of the most powerful incentives for getting something done is for a number of people to do it together, so they have prepared this book not only for couples to use alone but also to encourage them to join a couples' growth group. They describe those sponsored by the Association of Couples for Marriage Enrichment.

In addition to books already listed here and in the bibliography, several current books on marriage could be used: *Giving Time a Chance* by Ronna Romney and Beppie Harrison (New York: M. Evans, 1983); *The Secret of Staying in Love* by John Powell (Allen, Tex.: Argus Communications, 1974); *How to Choose the Wrong Marriage Partner and Live Unhappily Ever After* by Robert L. Mason and Carrie Jacobs (Atlanta: John Knox Press, 1979); *The Gift of Feeling* by Paul Tournier (Atlanta: John Knox Press, n.d.); and *Marriage Enrichment in the Church* by David and Vera Mace (Nashville: Broadman Press, 1977).

The church committee responsible for family education may elect to offer an annual marriage workshop led by a professional marriage counselor or professor of pastoral counseling. Or a professional counselor might be engaged to lead a series of seminars for newlyweds each

7. Mace and Mace, *How to Have a Happy Marriage* (Nashville: Abingdon Press, 1977), p. 30.

year, for which each couple would be charged a modest fee. Many young adults are taking advantage of adult education opportunities, for which they pay a fee. The church is missing an opportunity to make a marriage enrichment program possible if it does not offer courses, free or for a modest fee, from a Christian perspective. A fee may attract more couples and insure more faithful participation.

In conclusion, all ministry, both before and after the wedding ceremony, should be an expression of the church's concern, not merely the concern of the pastor. Ordinarily the pastor will take a leading role in developing this ministry. But the congregation and governing body should be involved in planning and in carrying through the plans. Otherwise the program will be viewed as the current pastor's "baby" to be thrown out when the pastor leaves, if it doesn't die earlier for lack of support.

Your congregation is looking to you, its pastor, to initiate ways in which pastor and people can render more effective ministry to couples.

3

MAKING THE SERVICE MORE PERSONAL

In recent years there has been increasing interest among couples preparing for marriage in writing either part or all of their wedding service. Some have involved family and friends in creating a wedding festival, complete with balloons, interspersed folk music, and colorful and unique costumes. The more usual personalizing of the wedding has consisted of writing the vows or involving the congregation in reading Scripture and poetry, singing processional and recessional hymns, and joining in litanies composed for the occasion. And there have been varying degrees of modification of the traditional liturgy.

The pastor will find some of the guidelines set forth in this chapter helpful in planning and performing ethnic weddings. Since customs vary greatly between ethnic groups, it is beyond the scope of this book to deal with them individually.

While a number of books provide resources and guidance for the couple in composing their wedding service, little has been written to guide the minister in the process of working with such couples. The present chapter attempts to meet this need.

Personalizing the Wedding Service

If the denomination's liturgy for the wedding service permits some leeway in the content and in the way the service is conducted, and most do, then the minister must decide whether to venture forth with a couple wishing to create their own unique service. If he or she is willing, the pastor can let this be known in the church's manual on weddings and receptions and also in the first counseling interview with couples preparing for marriage.

More often than not, couples who approach the minister with a request to assist them in writing their service are secure in their own sense of self-identity and social status. Such couples have a sincere desire to express their unique feelings and values in their ceremony.

When such a request is received, several factors must be considered: the denomination's teaching regarding the meaning of marriage, the denomination's liturgy, the time available for the couple and minister to work together, the openness of both sets of parents to anything other than the traditional wedding service, and the minister's own willingness to spend additional hours in counseling interviews and in planning for the personalized wedding. There should be a systems approach in the process of helping a couple write their service, since the many persons and factors involved will affect one another and the total outcome. The couple's families, the church, and the community at large have a vested interest in the success of this rite of passage.

If the couple does not have sufficient time to read, research, reflect, and work with the minister in writing their own service, then the minister should suggest that they choose one of the more contemporary services. Most services allow some flexibility and freedom in the selection of music, Scripture, wedding homily, Communion, gestures, and so on.

One campus chaplain requires five premarital interviews with any couple desiring to write their own wedding liturgy. The process of writing the vows and putting together the various parts of the ceremony can be a very useful counseling technique, since it demands that the prospective bride and groom think through the meaning of their commitment in greater depth than they otherwise might. Throughout the process of writing the wedding service, the minister should retain an influence over what is proposed and also should retain the freedom to refuse to conduct the service if the innovations proposed might alienate the couple's families or otherwise be destructive of their marriage.

The wise pastor will keep the proposed plans in the perspective of the overall view of the marriage and the meaning that such plans, if executed, might have for the couple many years later. In the intensity of emotion and excitement of romance, the couple may overlook this lasting effect.

Wedding liturgies, like other liturgies, may be classified as classical, contemporary, or experimental or free-wheeling. Examples of classical and contemporary services are found in Part II of this book. Experimental or free services are those written by the couple or borrowed elsewhere; the variations are infinite.

For many couples a contemporary wedding liturgy will provide the framework for the service they create. Written in contemporary English, using modern images and a more recent theology of marriage, the contemporary service lends itself to use by couples who want to break with the classical service but either do not wish to venture into creating an experimental liturgy or may be prevented by time or other factors from doing so. The contemporary service, for some, will be an adventure into the unfamiliar and risky area of liturgical innovation. For others, who are accustomed to contemporary worship services, it will seem familiar and comfortable.

Obviously, a couple wishing to create a unique service will need to be prepared to spend some time becoming familiar with the development of the wedding liturgy and the theology of Christian marriage and in reflecting upon what they want to say in and through their service. Such a service should have a unifying theme and liturgical integrity.

Few couples are able to do much homework in preparing an experimental wedding liturgy, thus very few such services are liturgically outstanding. While they may be festive and fun, they may, in the light of years, appear more like circuses than like religious celebrations. Joyful dignity can be attained in an experimental wedding liturgy, but only through careful reflection and planning.

Two trends in recent wedding liturgies should be especially encouraged. The revival of active participation by the congregation and wedding party in the service and the incorporation of the proclamation of the Word and celebration of the Eucharist are to be commended.

During the first three centuries, a civil marriage of baptized Christians was considered a Christian marriage. Tertullian (ca. A.D. 160–220) admonished Christians to celebrate the Eucharist at marriage services as a substitute for the Roman custom of sacrificing to Jupiter. For the first thousand years Christians followed secular customs but infused them with Christian meaning. Marriage was not officially designated a sacrament by the Roman Church until A.D. 1439. Protestant couples should be encouraged to plan their wedding services so that Christ is exalted, God is recognized as the giver of life, love, and marriage, and the unity of believers with one another and their God is celebrated. The wedding that includes the Word and Eucharist is ideal.

When a wedding homily or sermon is given, this should come early in the service, and the Communion should be celebrated as the climax, with the ceremony itself serving as the hinge on which the whole service of worship turns. The homily is usually given by the minister, but another member of the wedding party may be asked to do this. Scripture may be read by members of the wedding party or congregation. The bride and groom may read passages to each other, especially those selected from the Song of Solomon.

The wedding homily should set forth the biblical understanding of marriage. (The most important texts regarding marriage are found in Gen. 1:26-31; 2:18-25; 3:5-7, 15-20; Jesus' teaching in Matt. 19:5-15; Mark 10:2-16; Luke 16:18; and 1 Cor. 6:15-20; 7:1-40; 2 Cor. 11:2-4; Eph. 5:21–6:4; Rev. 19:6-16. Other biblical passages in which marriage symbolism is used to convey the mystic relation between God and his people are Song of Sol.; Isa. 54:5ff.; Jer. 31:31ff.; Hos. 2; and John 2:1-11; 3:20.)

In the Bible, marriage is understood as founded by God. It is a vocation. Men and women are called of God to be husband and wife and parents. In this sense marriages are made in heaven, although a particular marriage may not be. What God has joined together (the male-female relationship in marriage), human beings are not to put asunder.

In Matthew 19:4-6, Jesus reaffirms sexuality as part of the goodness of creation. He declares that the union of man and woman in their total being as "one flesh" is at the core of marriage. The wedding sermon should not be so "spiritual" that it denies this aspect of marriage.

The covenant character of marriage should be affirmed in the wedding homily or elsewhere in the service. As a holy covenant, Christian marriage implies a freely chosen, unconditional, lifelong, exclusive relationship. It cannot be stressed too strongly that marriage is based not on romantic love but on an *act of the will.* In *Divine Imperative,* Emil Brunner states that while marriage cannot be based on romantic love, God has made natural love an essential part of the order of marriage:

> It is true, of course, that marriage springs from love, but its stability is based not on love but on fidelity. Through the marriage vows the feeling of love is absorbed into the personal will; this alone provides the guarantee to the other party which justifies the venture of such a life companionship.[1]

There is no place in the Christian tradition for what is called term marriage or experimental marriage (this is different from an experimental *liturgy*). Such marriages

1. Brunner, *Divine Imperative* (Philadelphia: Westminster Press, 1947), pp. 357-58.

lack the most essential element of marriage — the obligation to be faithful. Marriage is primarily the personal concern of two people who love each other, feel drawn to each other by love, and express their feeling for each other by saying, "With you alone do I wish to be united, wholly, and as long as we both shall live." This vow to be faithful frees the partners to create an open, trusting relationship, not bound by an overconcern for their subjective feelings toward each other. Any attempt to modify permanence in marriage vows, implicitly or explicitly, should be vetoed by the minister. A vow to live as husband and wife as long as we both shall "love" instead of "live" implies a less than Christian understanding of marriage.

The couple and minister may want to read some wedding homilies to gain ideas for making the wedding more meaningful. A helpful model wedding sermon is Dietrich Bonhoeffer's "A Wedding Sermon from a Prison Cell," in *Letters and Papers from Prison.*[2] The wedding homily is an opportunity for the minister to venture a variety of sermon forms.

The wedding ceremony follows the Word proclaimed and is a response in action and words to God's gracious action and Word in Jesus Christ. The covenant made by bride and groom is a commitment to love each other in response to God's steadfast love revealed in Christ. Agape, unselfish and unmerited love, is the quality of love they are to share.

The Eucharist, when celebrated, climaxes the wedding service. It is truly a "thanksgiving" for God's gracious gift of

2. Bonhoeffer, *Letters and Papers from Prison* (New York: Macmillan, 1967), pp. 25-32.

marriage, for these two persons who have now entered the marriage relationship, and for God's providential guidance and care. In the Communion, Christ comes anew to renew the faithful. In the breaking of bread and pouring of the cup, God's covenant with his people is reenacted and renewed. And the steadfast love of God is given afresh to bride and groom to enable them to continue loving and forgiving each other as God loves and forgives them.

Resources

Most couples are not clear about what makes for a Christian service of worship. Several books can be helpful at this point. James F. White's *Introduction to Christian Worship* (Nashville: Abingdon Press, 1981) is an excellent book on worship in the Christian tradition and contains a very helpful section on the wedding service. *Doxology* by Geoffrey Wainwright (New York: Oxford University Press, 1980) is a systematic theology written from the perspective of worship. It would be good background reading for the more serious couple or for the minister interested in worship. Both of these books will help answer the questions, What is worship? and Why is it important to the Christian life?

Briefer essays on worship and the marriage service will be found in *Companion to the Book of Worship* of The United Methodist Church (William F. Dunkle, Jr., and Joseph D. Quillian [Nashville: Abingdon Press, 1970]), part of which was written by White. Chapter V, "The Order for the Service of Marriage" by Paul W. Hoon, treats the historical, pastoral, theological, and liturgical aspects of the marriage service.

Carl F. Schalk's pamphlet *Planning the Wedding Service*

is a helpful aid. (Order from Concordia Publishing House, 3558 S. Jefferson Ave., St. Louis, MO 63118.) Another booklet, *Creating the Christian Marriage,* is an extremely valuable guide for the couple creating an experimental service. It not only provides resources but also seeks to evoke from the couple what they want to express in their wedding celebration. By using their creativity, a couple can design a marriage festival that is fully representative of their combined individualities. This booklet shows a couple how to make it happen. (Order from Sacred Design, 840 Colorado Ave. S., Minneapolis, MN 55416.)

A very useful tool for the couple planning a wedding of any kind is *Your Wedding Workbook* by Natalia Belting and James R. Hine. It contains a checklist to use in planning the wedding. (Order from Interstate Printers, 19 Jackson St., Danville, IL 61832.)

Many resources contain poetry, music, and readings appropriate for Christian experimental wedding services. Criteria for evaluating such resources should be discussed by the minister and the couple. Does the poem or reading reflect a Christian understanding of love and marriage or a secular one? Is it appropriate for a service of Christian worship? Does it exalt Christ? Collections of contemporary as well as classical poetry can be found in the public library, and one can carefully select materials. Or one or more members of the wedding party may wish to compose a poem or song as a gift to the couple.

Any wedding service will be enhanced by a wedding service bulletin. In a "free" service, the bulletin is a necessity if the congregation and the wedding party are to follow and participate, unless the service is completely spontaneous. The bulletin contains the words to any songs, responses, litanies, and prayers in which the congregation is expected to join. It may also contain the couple's vows, names of members of the wedding party, new address and phone number of the couple, and names of clergy officiating. Everything needed for participation in the wedding service should be on *one* bulletin and should be simple to follow.

The Process Outlined

In the minister's first interview with the couple who wish to personalize their wedding service, they may be asked how they arrived at the decision to write some or all of their service, and what they have liked or disliked at other weddings they have attended. They may be assured that at this point everything is negotiable.

The minister should have on hand copies of various styles of wedding liturgies, including classical and contemporary. These and other examples of wedding services that the couple like may be shared and discussed.

It may seem paradoxical, but couples who write their own vows are usually more conservative in their concept of marriage than many who do not. Original vows in the bride's or groom's own words usually reflect a deeper and more personal commitment than do those that are merely repeated. The very fact that the couple wishes to "buy into" the forming of the service with their personal choices indicates a greater concern for making the wedding meaningful. *Choice heightens awareness.* Thus the process of decision making in creating all or part of a wedding service raises the level of consciousness of the persons involved.

After a number of interviews with the couple, the minister will be able to help them select a unifying theme for their wedding service. At this point they should be prepared to write out a rough draft of their vows. One couple went into separate rooms to do this. They did not reveal to each other what they had written until the vows were said in the service.

The vows are the heart of the wedding ceremony. In fact, the betrothal can be omitted, along with the ring ceremony. Or the ring ceremony can be combined with the vows so that the bride and groom place the rings on each other's fingers while making their vows. The vows may be read by the minister with the couple affirming "I do" or "I will," but it is preferable for them to say the vows to each other. They may memorize them, read them from the wedding bulletin or a card, or be prompted by the minister.

The marriage covenant is made by the bride and groom joining right hands and saying their vows. Vows should reflect a lifelong commitment that recognizes the negative as well as the positive aspects of life. The mature love and fidelity pledged should squarely face sickness, disappointment, and failure, which are inevitable in life. Some couples include a commitment to work together for social justice and world peace, recognizing their responsibility not only to each other but also to society. And some pledge to love and support the children they have now or may have in the future.

After the vows are written, the wedding ceremony is shaped around them. The selection of music, prayers, Scripture, poetry, and litanies should reflect the theme of the wedding expressed in the vows.

When a rough draft of the entire wedding ceremony is completed the couple should be asked if their parents are "in" or "out" of the wedding plans, if this has not already been determined. If they are "in," a copy of the rough draft should be sent to parents. Some couples may want to ask for comments. This approach allows parents to participate in planning the wedding service, especially if it is an unconventional one. If the bride's mother knows ahead of time that there will be no traditional wedding processional, she will not be shocked at the wedding, although she may not be happy with the substitute.

The wedding should serve to *strengthen,* not weaken, family ties. In fact, the couple may want to dramatize the uniting of their two families by inviting both sets of parents to join them in the chancel when the bride arrives there. The parents may give the bride and groom to each other and join hands for a moment as a new, larger family. A parent or parents may make a brief statement recognizing the bride and groom as adults and welcoming the new son and daughter into the family.

The wedding is a rite of passage, the sign of persons moving from one way of life to another. No one moves easily from one form of life to another. A time of affirmation of family ties during the event can make the rite of passage easier for all involved. Gestures and words can make it even more meaningful.

The pronouncement of the couple as husband and wife and the giving of the blessing on their marriage will be done, of course, by the minister. But the couple may wish to discuss it and offer suggestions. With the pronouncement, many ministers address the couple with words of admonition and counsel before giving the blessing. Some give them a verse of Scripture to guide them in their new relationship.

Another gesture that has become popular is a candle-lighting ceremony. This can effectively dramatize the meaning of the rite of passage. There are several ways in which it may be done. The bride and groom, each carrying a taper, move to opposite ends of the altar. Each lights a taper from a large candle there, blows out the candle, and both move to the center of the altar, where they light a single large candle. If this seems to ring too much of marriage-as-disappearance-of-self, the couple may light the two altar candles together. The candles may be their gift to the church, or the church's gift to them. The candles serve as reminders of Christ, the Light of the world, who blesses Christian marriage: "The two shall be one flesh." As the couple go through the actions of lighting candles the minister may wish to read appropriate passages of Scripture and interpret their actions for the congregation.

The "kiss of peace" is another gesture being used in wedding services. An ancient ritual of Christian love, this custom is usually performed by a double handclasp and words such as "Peace be with you, Jan," and the reply, "And with your spirit, George." Bride and groom may pass the peace to members of the congregation after their vows or at the conclusion of the service. It is especially appropriate at the conclusion of a Communion that climaxes a wedding service.

You, the minister, have been asked by the couple to help them make their wedding service the most meaningful event of their lives. They look to you for guidance, counsel, and support. And they are counting on you to see that what you three have planned together *happens* in their wedding service.

4

CONDUCTING THE SERVICE

The Christian wedding, whether celebrated privately in a home or publicly in church, should be planned and conducted as a service of worship, not a performance. Christ, not the bride or the couple, should be the focus of the Christian wedding. Those who elect to have a Christian ceremony rather than a civil wedding service should expect to be guided by the Scriptures and church traditions rather than by current fads.

Before conducting a wedding service, a minister should become informed regarding the marriage laws of the particular state in which the wedding is to take place. Some states require that the minister be bonded. Others require a certain waiting period. In some states laws vary by county. The minister should make certain that the marriage license was issued in the county in which the wedding is to take place, when this is required. *And the completed wedding license should be delivered promptly by mail or in person to the proper civil authority.*

The wedding rehearsal and ceremony are under the *sole direction* of the minister. The 1993 edition of the *Book of Common Worship* of the Presbyterian Church (U.S.A.) states: "As a service of Christian worship, the marriage service is under the direction of the minister and the supervision of the Session." In the interview to plan the wedding service the minister should inform the bride if the assistance of a florist or bridal consultant in conducting the rehearsal and wedding is needed. If not, this should be made clear to the bride so there will be no misunderstanding at the rehearsal or the wedding.

While many bridal consultants can offer valuable assistance in positioning the bridal party in the chancel and in starting the members of the processional at the proper time, this function can also be performed by an experienced member of the church's altar guild or worship committee. If the minister chooses to accept the assistance of a bridal consultant, the function that the consultant is to perform should be made clear before the rehearsal.

The wedding policy statement of one church states: "The rector and church organist always direct the rehearsal. They will welcome suggestions, but their word will be final. *No professional bridal consultant will be present at the rehearsal.* The rector and organist have found from experience that the rehearsal and the wedding will go more smoothly if no professional bridal consultant is present. A member of the Altar Guild will be present at both the rehearsal and the wedding to help the wedding party. *The bride should expect to take the part of the bride in the rehearsal.*" Another church's policy states that all requests for type of service and changes in service, including positioning of the bridal party, must be made in consultation with the minister prior to the time of the rehearsal.

If the minister chooses to direct the rehearsal and wedding without assistance from a bridal consultant or florist, he or she should meet with the bride and groom in the place where the wedding will be held to make notes regarding their preferences in conducting the processional, ceremony, and recessional. *This is essential if the rehearsal is to go smoothly.* There is nothing more frustrating than attempting to conduct a large rehearsal with too many directors. One bridal consultant indicated that she preferred leaving the entire direction to the minister, but that she knew of only three ministers who could direct a rehearsal smoothly. She emphasized the necessity of prior planning.

The minister functions in the wedding as director, prompter, and participant. As director, it is helpful to have the advice of a recent book on wedding etiquette as well as the denominational worship book. Books on social etiquette include chapters on wedding etiquette.

Flexibility and creativity characterize weddings today more than in the past. The desire of a couple to personalize their wedding service need not be cause for resistance or alarm on the part of either family or minister.

The Rehearsal

Rehearsal of the wedding ceremony has become a standard procedure for all weddings, except for small private affairs. The rehearsal is usually held the day before or two days before the wedding. Late afternoon, *before* the rehearsal dinner, is the most popular time. This allows for a leisurely dinner.

Unfortunately there is a temptation on the part of some members of wedding parties to clown around during the rehearsal. This is especially common when the rehearsal follows a dinner where there has been drinking.

If begun on time and if there are no hitches, the rehearsal should take no longer than thirty to forty-five minutes.

The rehearsal should be held in the place where the wedding will take place. All members of the wedding party, including the bride, should rehearse. In the last interview with the couple the minister should ask them to urge all members of the wedding party to arrive on time. The organist should be on hand, although soloists and other musicians may rehearse with the organist at another time. This is preferred, since it shortens the time needed for the rehearsal.

The rehearsal begins when the minister asks all members of the wedding party to sit in the front pews. The pastor may want to welcome those who are not members of the congregation. In order to set the tone of the rehearsal, something like this may be said to help create an atmosphere of cooperation and joyful dignity:

> We are gathered here to rehearse the wedding service of our friends Jan and George. If each of us will listen carefully to instructions and learn our parts well, we will be comfortable in our roles during the wedding. We will rehearse the service as many times as necessary for you to be certain of your part. Usually thirty to forty-five minutes is sufficient. Please feel free to ask any questions you may have.
>
> Let us bow our heads for prayer as we ask God's guidance and blessing.
>
> Gracious God, thank you for allowing us to share the happiness of Jan and George as they prepare to be married. Guide us that we may contribute our best to you and to them in the ceremony. May the Spirit of the Living Christ infect us with joy as we now prepare for the celebration of their marriage. Bless us we humbly pray. Amen.

After the opening prayer the minister may want to give a brief overview of the rehearsal:

> The wedding ceremony is a worship service in the Christian tradition. God has ordained marriage, and Jesus blessed marriage by his presence at the wedding at Cana. As we rehearse we may think of the wedding as a little drama consisting of three acts. Act 1 is the processional, Act 2 is the ceremony itself, and Act 3 is the recessional. Contrary to the usual practice in rehearsing a drama, the wedding is best rehearsed by beginning with Act 3! Then we move to Act 1, the processional, and then Acts 2 and 3. Let us begin by taking our proper places in the chancel. First, will Jan and George please come take their places, with George on my left and Jan on my right? Next, will Jan's maid of honor take her place on Jan's left? And now will the best man take his place on George's right? The bridesmaids will please come forward and take their places to my right, and the ushers will take their places to my left. (The father of the bride will have been seated earlier in the service.)

Now the bridesmaids and ushers should be positioned. Their positions should have been planned earlier by the minister and couple and sketched out on a diagram, with the names of each written in. They may be arranged in ascending or descending order of height from the bride or alternating tall and short. They need not be in a straight line but may alternate forward and behind or may be arranged in an arc. The arrangement of the chancel, number in the wedding party, and preference of the couple will determine the arrangement. It may be necessary to make some minor changes at the rehearsal in order to achieve the desired effect. The following diagrams illustrate two possible arrangements.

Church with Center Aisle

FRONT

C

B B B B MH   BM U U U U

1 BR G

2 1   3 4

Bride's Side   Groom's Side

B: Bridesmaids
MH: Maid of Honor

C: Clergy
BR: Bride
G: Groom

BM: Best Man
U: Ushers

1: Bride's Father
2: Bride's Mother

3: Groom's Father
4: Groom's Mother

Church without Center Aisle

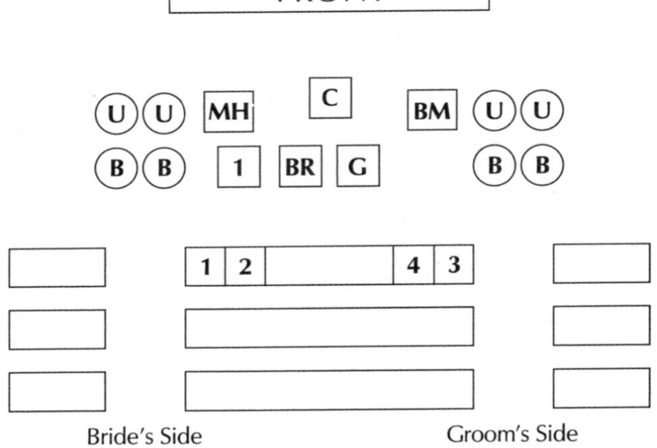

U: Ushers
B: Bridesmaids
MH: Maid of Honor

C: Clergy
BR: Bride
G: Groom

BM: Best Man
U: Ushers
B: Bridesmaids

1: Bride's Father
2: Bride's Mother

3: Groom's Father
4: Groom's Mother

If the bride, maid of honor, groom, best man, and minister(s) are to advance farther toward the altar after the bride has been presented, this final position should now be taken. It is from this position that the recessional will begin. Each person should be asked to observe carefully where he or she is standing. During the rehearsal it may be helpful to place hymnbooks or other objects on the floor to mark the places for bridesmaids and ushers. By the end of the rehearsal they should have learned their positions in relation to the chancel furniture and each other so that they will not need to be marked.

The minister now signals to the organist to begin the recessional music, and the entire wedding party recesses to the rear of the church. The order for the recessional is as follows: bride and groom, ring bearer and flower girl, maid of honor (either alone or on arm of best man or usher). In an ultraformal wedding the best man follows the minister to the minister's study to present the fee entrusted to him by the groom. It is optional whether the bridesmaids recess alone or on arms of ushers. The ushers follow if they do not escort the bridesmaids. Any ushers not escorting bridesmaids recess in pairs. If the bridesmaids processed in pairs, they may also recess in pairs, followed by the ushers in pairs.

When the ceremony is climaxed by a celebration of the Lord's Supper, the wedding party may be seated on the front pews or special chairs during the sacrament; or they may choose to remain standing depending upon the size of the congregation and the circumstances. And during a lengthy homily, the wedding party may be seated.

In some weddings the bride and groom wish to be present for the wedding music. In this case the wedding party would not process in but would take their places in the front pews or in chairs in the chancel area. The form of the wedding service will determine the preferable arrangement and procedure.

Now the processional is practiced. The groom and best man go to the door through which they will enter with the minister. The bride, bride's father, and other members of the bridal party take their places at the rear of the church. Someone will be needed to start them at the right time. A friend of the family, bridal consultant, member of the altar guild, etc., may do this. This person should make a list of the persons in the order in which they are to process. The minister or wedding director signals to the organist to begin the processional. The minister, groom, and best man, in that order, come in and take their places at the head of the aisle, where they await the bridal party. When the minister is in place, the ushers enter from the same entrance used by the minister or from the rear of the sanctuary. In a church with two aisles, ushers may enter by one and bridesmaids by the other. The ushers may enter by twos or may escort a bridesmaid. When the ushers reach their positions at the chancel they turn to face the center aisle and stand with their hands at their sides, or folded in front with left over right, or behind them. But all should follow the same pattern. They should be encouraged to smile pleasantly as the other members of the wedding party process.

The bridesmaids enter next, spaced about fifteen feet apart on a long aisle, ten to twelve feet apart on a short aisle. In a large wedding they may enter in pairs. They are followed by the maid of honor, ring bearer, and flower girl. The flower girl is *always* the last to process before the bride.

The bride and her father (or male relative) enter next,

with the father on her left. They pause for a moment at the head of the center aisle so that the "starter" can straighten her train. The organist signals the entrance of the bride with a joyous crescendo. The bride and her father begin on the left foot and process, keeping in step. It is optional for the congregation to stand for the processional. If they stand, the minister should gesture when they are to stand and when they are to be seated.

The bride, on the arm of her father, proceeds to the center of the aisle and stops about two feet in front of the minister. The organ fades out promptly.

The minister may then read through all or key parts of the wedding service. It is helpful if the names the bride and groom wish to use in their vows have been written on a slip of paper and paperclipped to the servicebook. (In some areas middle names are very important.)

The minister's question of the bride's father, "Who presents this woman to be wed?" is the signal for the bride to release her father's arm and transfer the bouquet from her right to her left hand. The bride's father may answer the question by silently — or with the words "I do" or "Her mother and I do" — placing the bride's right hand in the right hand of the minister. The father is then seated by the bride's mother, next to the aisle. If the congregation has been standing, it may be seated at this point.

The minister then places the bride's right hand in the groom's right hand. Bride and groom face each other. If the vows are to be said farther up toward the altar, the minister, bride, groom, maid of honor, and best man move to their new positions before the minister places the bride's hand in the groom's. The bride may steady herself on the arm of the groom as they move.

In rehearsing the vows in a large sanctuary, it is a good idea for someone in the rear to listen to determine whether the vows can be heard. If they cannot, the bride and groom should raise the level of their voices. They should look into each other's eyes while making this solemn covenant. After the groom says his vow, the couple loose hands and the bride takes the groom's right hand in hers as she says her vow to him.

Then the bride gives her flowers to the maid of honor for the ring ceremony. The best man either will have received the ring for the bride before the service began or will have received it from the ring bearer at the end of the processional. If it is a double-ring ceremony, the maid of honor holds the ring for the groom. The rings can be carried safely on the attendants' fingers until needed. If a ring is accidentally dropped the best man should rescue it. If the bride wears gloves, either she should remove the left glove or the third finger of the glove should be cut off beforehand. The bride wears her engagement ring on her right hand, and after the service she places it on her left hand over the wedding band.

The best man gives the ring to the minister, who offers a prayer of blessing and gives it to the groom. As the groom places it on the bride's finger, he says the ring vow. Next the maid of honor gives the groom's ring to the minister, who offers a prayer of blessing and gives it to the bride. (This transfer of rings is easily done if the ring is placed in the palm of the minister's hand and taken from the palm.) The bride places the ring on the groom's finger as she says the ring vow.

When there is a prayer bench, sometimes referred to as a prie-dieu, the couple kneels for prayer. Otherwise they remain standing as the minister offers a prayer, followed by the Lord's Prayer. Many ministers feel that the Lord's Prayer should be the first prayer said together by the new husband and wife and the congregation and should *not* be sung as a solo.

The couple then stands. The minister declares them husband and wife, asks them to again join right hands, places the end of the stole on or around their joined hands, thus "tying the knot," and says, "Whom God has joined together . . ."

The minister pronounces the benediction. The couple may choose to kneel for the benediction if they did not kneel earlier. If kneeling, they now stand. At this point the couple may kiss. While most church rituals omit the kiss, there is historical and theological basis for it. There is evidence of the kiss at the betrothal, which is now combined with the marriage vows, as early as the third century.[1] In *Experiencing God: Theology as Spirituality,* Kenneth Leech tells us that

> in Old Testament times, covenants were established between individuals, between husbands and wives, between tribes, between monarchs, or between a ruler and his people. When such a covenant was established, there were rights and duties on both sides, and covenants were sealed by gifts, by a kiss or a handshake, or by the sharing of a common meal.[2]

1. See Kenneth Stevenson, *Nuptial Blessing* (New York: Oxford University Press, 1983), p. 19.

2. Leech, *Experiencing God: Theology as Spirituality* (San Francisco: Harper & Row, 1985), p. 68.

Some couples prefer to postpone the kiss until later, in the rear of the church, rather than make a public display of their affection. The wedding kiss may be seen as a sign of incorporation and a symbol of sexual union that unites husband and wife into one body.

The "Service of Christian Marriage" of The United Methodist Church indicates that at this point in the service "the couple and minister(s) may greet each other, after which greetings may be exchanged throughout the congregation." Members of the congregation may greet one another with handclasps, embraces, kisses, and/or verbal greetings such as "The peace of Christ be with you."

In the early church the kiss was exchanged by Christians as a symbol of Christian love. Although erotic by nature, the wedding kiss by the bride and groom should not be overly long or dramatic but expressed in good taste. The minister may want to advise the couple on the proper procedure at the rehearsal.

The maid of honor gives the bride her bouquet and helps straighten her train. Then the bride takes her husband's right arm as they prepare to recess to the rear of the church. The organist begins the recessional music, and the recessional continues as rehearsed earlier.

The processional should now be rehearsed again. Check with the organist to see if he or she is comfortable with the procedure and timing. Ask members of the wedding party if they have any questions and if they are comfortable with their roles.

With the wedding party in place, any or all of the ceremony may be practiced as is felt necessary. The bride and groom should practice clasping their right hands as they face each other to exchange vows. Emphasize the eye contact as they make this solemn covenant before God and witnesses.

The exchange of rings should be practiced until it can be done with ease. In the rehearsal and during the wedding, the minister may want to comment on the meaning of this gesture. It reflects older symbolic exchanges of property and the endowing of each other with all their worldly goods. The ring, made of precious metal, symbolizes the purity of the love they are to share. The circular shape of the ring symbolizes their love, which has no end, and which they pledge to each other "until death do us part."

If the bride and groom choose to kneel for prayer, this also should be practiced. The maid of honor should be coached to take care of the bride's dress and train so that she can rise without difficulty. The bride may want to practice giving her bouquet to her maid of honor and receiving it. And the maid of honor may want to practice lifting the veil and straightening the train.

Then reassemble the wedding party in the front pews. Let the ushers practice their roles by seating bridesmaids as if they were guests. The ushers should be instructed to ask guests whether they are relatives of the bride or groom. The bride's relatives are seated on the left side of the church and the groom's relatives on the right side, within spaces reserved by ribbons. If guests are not relatives of either bride or groom, ushers should attempt to seat them so that the sanctuary is balanced, with about as many guests on one side as the other. Ushers may need to be shown how to extend their right arm for women to hold as they are led to a seat, while the husbands and children follow. The ushers who are to seat the bride's mother and groom's mother and any grandmothers should be assigned, and this may be practiced. The groom's grandmothers are seated first, then the bride's, then the groom's mother, and the bride's mother last. Then the aisle runner, if used, is unrolled. Aisle runners are carryovers from days when dresses became soiled in the aisles.

The ushers who are to light the candles should practice this procedure, making sure they know where the tapers are located. They should be cautioned to make sure each candle is well lighted, working in unison from the outside of the candelabras toward the center. They should also be reminded to extinguish the candles as soon as the pictures are taken after the ceremony.

The usual procedure for the wedding service is as follows:

1. prelude music (timed by the organist so that the bride can process at the hour announced for the wedding)
2. seating of guests by ushers
3. candles lighted
4. groom's parents seated
5. bride's mother seated
6. aisle runner laid
7. vocal or other music
8. wedding processional
9. marriage ceremony
10. recessional
11. bride's grandparents and parents ushered out, followed by groom's grandparents and parents
12. congregation dismissed by minister.

The person who serves as the "starter" will need to alert the ushers when it is time to light the candles, seat mothers, lay the runner, usher out parents, and extinguish candles.

Before dismissing the rehearsal, make certain everyone knows the place and time he or she is to appear for the wedding. Ushers normally arrive an hour before the service begins. If the wedding party dresses at the church, everyone may want to arrive an hour before the wedding.

The groom should give the minister the marriage license *at the rehearsal.* The minister should review it to make sure it is in order. If witnesses are required, the minister should alert the best man and maid of honor to sign the license after the wedding. If the state does not provide a marriage certificate, the minister may want to have a supply of such certificates on hand. They can be purchased from church supply houses. The certificate should be filled in, signed, and given to the couple before they leave.

Variations

The Double Wedding

The double wedding is similar, except that two bridegrooms follow the minister and stand side by side, each with his best man behind him. The groom of the older bride should be nearer the aisle. Ushers of both bridegrooms go up the aisle together. The bridesmaids of the older bride, followed by her maid of honor, enter next. The older bride follows on the right arm of her father or other relative. Next in order come the bridesmaids of the younger bride, her maid of honor, and finally the younger bride, on the arm of a brother, uncle, or other relative.

When There Are Two or More Ministers

The bride's own pastor should be asked to perform the wedding unless a parent or close relative of the couple is a minister. In that case the bride asks her pastor to invite the relative to conduct the service and invites her pastor to assist. Other ministers may be asked to assist the bride's pastor, and the invitation should be extended through that pastor. The two ministers confer and divide the wedding ceremony leadership between them. Usually the assisting minister leads the first part of the service through the question to the bride's father. Then the minister in charge takes the service from that point on. The assisting minister may lead the Lord's Prayer and give the benediction. When there are additional ministers the leadership of the service may be similarly shared.

Wedding of a Minister

Traditional professional courtesy among ministers calls for ministers performing the wedding of another minister or ministers to return any honorarium to the couple. Or the minister may tell the couple in the first counseling session that she or he would like to perform the wedding gratis. However, reimbursement for expenses incurred for travel and entertainment may be accepted.

Wedding of a Minister's Daughter

When the bride's father is a clergyman, she may ask him to perform the ceremony and also present her. Or she may ask a brother or other male relative to present her. But if she wishes to have her father present her and also perform the service, she may ask another minister to conduct the first part of the service through the question to the bride's father. After presenting his daughter in marriage, the minister then moves to a new position from which he conducts the remainder of the service.

If the bride's mother is a minister and is asked to perform the ceremony, this is done in the usual fashion. Here the seating of the groom's mother is the signal for the processional to begin. The bride's father presents the bride and takes a seat in the front pew.

If both parents are ministers, appropriate responsibilities should be agreed upon in the early planning stages.

Variations because of Personal Preferences

Each wedding is different because of personal preferences. One couple chose to hear the music at their wedding. They entered from separate places, sat together with their wedding party in the front of the church, then took their places for the ceremony. When the wedding follows a regular congregational service of worship, which is becoming more frequent, the couple and their attendants may take their places for the ceremony without processing. Other variations are discussed in Chapter 3, "Making the Service More Personal."

The Home or Garden Wedding

The same procedure is followed for the processional as in the church wedding. In the home wedding, the wedding party proceeds down the stairs to the place where the service is to be performed. In a garden wedding they proceed from the house to the place where the ceremony is to be conducted. A prayer bench may be used if desired. In small private home weddings, the processional is eliminated.

After the ceremony there is no recessional. When the minister withdraws at the conclusion of the service, the bride and groom merely turn to receive congratulations from their guests. When there is no recessional the bride and groom always kiss before they turn to receive their guests.

The Marriage Ceremony in the Minister's Home or Study

The bride and groom usually come to the minister's home or study together and are met there by their families and a few invited friends. The minister reads the service and the couple are congratulated afterward by family and friends. They then proceed to the place of the reception.

The Blessing of a Civil Marriage

This service is similar to the regular service, except that at the beginning of the service it is announced that the man and woman have already been married by the laws of the state. (See "The Blessing of a Civil Marriage" in Part II, pp. 158-62.)

The Wedding as Part of a Regular Worship Service

It is becoming more common for couples to be married during "concerns and celebrations" time or at the end of a regular congregational worship service. There is good church tradition to support this practice.

5

MUSIC AND THE WEDDING

In most churches the minister will refer the bride and groom to the church organist for help in selecting appropriate music. A well-trained musician with a biblical foundation and an understanding of the place of music in the church's life can be a real asset, but the minister also can give the couple some guidance.

Problems regarding the choice of music for weddings usually arise with couples coming from the fringe of the church's life. Persons nurtured in the church have a greater concern that the music reflect a Christian understanding of marriage, but those on the fringe may ask for music of a thoroughly secular nature. Music from Broadway hits or popular movies is, unfortunately, used in some weddings today.

In guiding the couple in the choice of wedding music, the minister may want to raise the basic question, "Why have a church wedding?" This question naturally leads to the next: "What do I do to express the reason why I have come to church to be married?" The minister can ask these questions without judging the couple and their motives.

Music speaks for its age and reflects its age. Couples considering particular pieces of music should be encouraged to ask, "Is this music lifting up the life-style and values I want to emphasize?" Each couple must reach their own answer, but they should do it with integrity.

The church wedding service is the church at worship and the church in witness, and the music should contribute to Christian worship and witness. Some of the people who come to weddings seldom, if ever, attend regular church services. The entire wedding service, but especially the choice and performance of the music, can be a credit to the church's worship and witness.

Music that is associated with certain words is easier to evaluate than music that has no words. The latter can be judged only on the symbolic level. This can be tricky for the layperson, and a trained musician is needed to guide the couple. But when there are words associated with the music, they should be judged on the basis of their appropriateness for a service of Christian worship.

Most ministers feel (and I feel emphatically) that the words to music used in a church wedding should not be humanistic or Gnostic. Gnostic music says that the world has a problem, but if we just love a little more we can, by our own efforts, make the world better. Humanistic music has no transcendental reference: Human love, but especially romantic love, is all we need for success in marriage. Neither Gnostic nor humanistic songs lead to a deeper faith in God and reliance upon him for love, forgiveness, and life. Music at a wedding needs to be centered on God and God's action in the ceremony, rather than on the couple's feelings about each other.

Many churches have allowed secular music to become associated with church weddings. "Because," "I Love You Truly," "O Promise Me," "One Hand, One Heart," "The

Impossible Dream," "Through the Years," and "One Alone" are among the best known.

Most ministers also feel (and I am in full agreement) that traditional wedding marches are inappropriate and were never intended for use in a religious ceremony. The "Bridal Chorus" from Wagner's *Lohengrin,* for example, is associated with the parody "Here Comes the Bride." In the opera it occurs after the wedding, in an atmosphere of distrust and hatred concluded by death and separation. Another example, Mendelssohn's recessional march from "Incidental Music," was written for *A Midsummer Night's Dream* by Shakespeare; it was played before Act 4, in which Bottom, the weaver, is turned into an ass and produces clowning and foolishness. Furthermore, both pieces were originally written for full orchestra, not for the organ.

Since the chief reason for having a church wedding rather than a civil one is to acknowledge the Christian significance of marriage, it follows that *any music used in a church wedding should be worthy of the worship of Almighty God.* Instrumental music should evoke the spirit of prayer or praise. Any vocal texts should be God-centered, not human-centered. Such music expresses the joyful gratitude of the couple and their guests for God's gift of love. It also conveys a sense of reverence for the sacred relationship into which the bride and groom have been called.

The music selected for the wedding service should not be considered "cover" for the seating of guests or entertainment before the main event. Rather, it should set the mood of worship. Vocal selections, if used, should point up the religious significance of this great step in the lives of the bride and groom.

The church wedding, in contrast to a civil marriage service, is an occasion of *corporate* worship. The service should be one of *participation,* not observation. The bride and groom should be encouraged to involve the congregation in worship through the use of hymns, responses, and corporate prayers. The Lord's Prayer should be prayed by the congregation and wedding party, not sung as a solo.

There is a trend away from vocal soloists in church weddings. The minister of music of a large metropolitan church reports that during one summer, vocalists were used in only two of fifteen church weddings for which he played. In other recent summers, no vocalists were used. However, choirs are increasingly being used to lead congregational singing and for special music.

The prenuptial music need not be limited to the organ or piano. The harp, harpsichord, flute, violin, bell choir, trombone, clarinet, flute, trumpet, guitar, and chamber music ensembles are being used effectively in church weddings. The music chosen should be selected for the contribution it will make to the total worship service. It should reflect the joy of the occasion, avoiding music of a funereal character.

Prenuptial music should consist of contrasts — meditative tunes interspersed with sprightly louder melodies. The music selected may represent many periods. The bride and groom should allow the musician some leeway in selecting music with which she or he feels comfortable and which is suitable for the particular instrument. The musician's education and experience need to be honored. It is important that the musician have the support and backing of the minister in these choices. The European custom of leaving the selection of wedding music entirely to the musician would be desirable in many instances. The training and musical insight of the church organist should guide the couple rather than current fads and their preconceived ideas of what wedding music should consist of.

The bride and groom often have some particular song which has become "their" song during courtship. Frequently the bride wants "their" song played at the wedding. But unless it can pass the test of music fitting for a Christian worship service, it should be reserved for a social gathering. Sentimental love songs or semiclassics can add to the enjoyment of a rehearsal dinner or a reception. But they do not belong in a service of Christian worship.

One church's wedding brochure to guide couples sets forth the following policy:

> Because the ceremony is set in the context of worship, the music used in the wedding is expected to be religious. This automatically eliminates certain vocal numbers which are used in some weddings. As an aid to the bride the following music is suggested for consideration. If some number is desired which is not listed here, the request may be submitted to the Session's Committee on Worship through the minister.

The music listed in this brochure does not, of course, include the traditional Wagner processional and Mendelssohn recessional. The brochure encourages the use of a wedding bulletin and congregational participation in hymns, responsive readings, and prayers.

Announcements of the wedding in the church newsletter and in the newspaper might indicate that "Prenuptial music begins at _____ P.M., followed by wedding ceremony at _____ P.M." The hour given for the ceremony indicates the time the bride starts down the aisle. Guests should plan to arrive in time for the prenuptial music.

A church should have several resources on hand to give to couples. Many useful suggestions will be found in the appendix that follows.

APPENDIX 1:

SUGGESTED WEDDING MUSIC

Wedding Music Collections

Epley, Linda, and William Epley. *Music and Your Wedding.* Nashville: Southern Baptist Convention Sunday School Board.

Folk Songs for Weddings. Carol Stream, Ill.: Hope Publishing Co. Wide range of quality.

Fryxell. *Wedding Music.* Philadelphia: Fortress Press.

Johnson, David N., ed. *Wedding Music,* 5 vols. Minneapolis: Augsburg. An excellent resource for prenuptial, processional, and recessional music of all periods. Volume 2 includes music for use with B-flat instruments.

Krapf, Gerhard. *In Christian Love: Organ Music for Weddings and General Use.* Sacred Music Press, KK-435.

Krause, Paul. *Planning a Christian Wedding.* St. Louis: Concordia.

Langley, Robin, ed. *Classical Organ Music: From the Death of J. S. Bach to the Advent of Mendelssohn,* vol. 2. Oxford Press.

List of Music for the Wedding Service. Louisville: Office of Worship of the Presbyterian Church (U.S.A.). Includes appropriate suggestions for use with organ, instruments without organ, handbells, and choral music. Ministers and church musicians will find this a valuable resource.

Music for Church Weddings. Greenwich: Seabury Press.
Wedding Music, 2 vols. St. Louis: Concordia. An invaluable source of wedding music for church musicians.

Suggested Prenuptial Organ Music

(*Denotes easier organ selections)

Bach, J. S./Grace (arr.)	"Be Thou Near Me"
Bach, J. S.	"Blessed Jesus We Are . . ."
Bach, J. S.	"Jesu, Joy of Man's Desiring"
Bach, J. S.	"Let All Together Praise Our God"
Bach, J. S.	"Sheep and Lambs May Safely Graze"
Boyce, William	Voluntary in D Major
Brown, Christopher	Nocturne
Correll, Janet	Festival Prelude on "Coronation"
DuBois, Theodore	"Cantilena Nuptiale"
Frescobaldi	Introduction and Toccata
Gardner, John	"Dominus Regit Me"
Handel, G. F.	"Thanks Be to Thee"
Howells, Herbert	Siciliano
Hustad, Don	Voluntary on "O Perfect Love"
Jacob (arr.)	"Brother James' Air"
Jongen	Chorale
*Kee, Cor	Variations on "A Mighty Fortress"
*Mendelssohn, Felix	Adagio from the Sonata in F Minor

*Peeters, Flor	"Aria"
Reger	"Benedictus"
Schneider	"Our Father, Thou in Heaven Above"
Stanley, J.	Voluntaries
Vaughan Williams, Ralph	"Rhosymedre"
Vierne, Louis	Carillon de Westminster
Vierne, Louis	"Rhosymedre, Lied"
Walther	"Lord Jesus Christ Be Present Now"
Wright, Searle	"Brother James' Air"
Young, Gordon	Voluntary on "Kremser"

In addition, the following may be used:

- Adagio movements from organ symphonies such as those by Widor and Vierne
- Chorale preludes in *Wedding Music,* volume 2 (published by Concordia)
- Handel's organ concertos or sonatas
- Chorale preludes based on appropriate hymns of praise.

Or selections from these collections could be used:

- *Four Slow Movements from Sonatas by Mendelssohn* (published by Augsburg)
- *Music for Worship (With Easy Pedals)* by David Johnson.

PROCESSIONALS

Barr, John G.	"Processional Trumpet"
Beethoven, Ludwig von/H. Hopson	"Procession of Joy"

Boellmann	Chorale from *Suite Gothic*
Campra, Andre	"Rigaudon"
Clark, Jeremiah	"Prince of Denmark's March"*
Clark, Jeremiah	Trumpet Tunes of Jeremiah Clark
Drahman, Jean	Wedding Processional in F
Guilmant, Alexandre	Processional March
Handel, G. F.	Air from the *Water Music*
Handel, G. F.	Processional in G Major
Hopson, Hal	Procession in C Major
Hustad, Don	Processional on "Lauda Anima"
Johnson, David N.	Processional in E-flat
Mouret, Jean P.	Rondeau
Purcell, Henry	Trumpet Tunes
Shaw, Martin	Processional
Stanley, John	Trumpet Voluntary
Walton, William	"Crown Imperial"
Wetzler, R.	Processional on "Westminster Abbey"

In addition, familiar hymns such as the following may be used:

"All Creatures . . ."	Tune: Lasst uns erfreuen
"Joyful, Joyful, We Adore Thee"	Tune: Hymn to Joy
"Love Divine, All Loves Excelling"	Tune: Hyfrydol
"Praise to the Lord, the Almighty"	Tune: Lobe Den Herren

*Commonly known as Trumpet Voluntary by Henry Purcell.

Recessionals

Bach, J. S.	"In Thee Is Gladness"
Boellmann	Chorale from *Suite Gothic*
Handel, G. F.	Allegro Maestoso from the *Water Music*
Handel, G. F.	Allegro Moderato
Handel, G. F.	Postlude in G
Handel, G. F.	"The Rejoicing"
Hustad, Don	Recessional on "Nun Danket"
Karg-Elert	"Now Thank We All Our God"
Lang, C. S.	Tuba Tune in D Major
Leighton, Kenneth	"Fanfare"
Lemmens, Jacques	"Fanfare"
Mouret, Jean Joseph	Rondeau
Polley, David	"A Mighty Fortress"
Purcell, Henry	Trumpet Tunes
Schack, David	Chorale Prelude on "All Glory Be to God Alone"
Stanley, John	Trumpet Voluntary
Sullivan, Michael	Postlude and Chorale on "Grosser Gott"
Vaughan Williams, Ralph	"Hyfrydol"
Widor, Charles	Toccata from Symphony #5
Willian, Healey	"Epithalame" (Sortie)
Zipoli, Domenico	"Festival Postlude"

In addition to "Now Thank We All Our God," other hymns may be used, such as the following:

"O God, Our Help in Ages Past" Tune: St. Anne

Suggested Vocal Music

Bach, J. S.	"Jesu, Joy of Man's Desiring"*
Bach, J. S.	"Jesus Shepherd, Be Thou Near Me"
Bach, J. S.	"O Love That Casts Out Fear"
Busarow, Donald	"Love Is the Sunlight"
Busarow, Donald	"When Jesus to the Wedding Went"
Fetler	"O Father, All Creating"
Franck, C.	"O Lord Most Holy"
Gounod	"Entreat Me Not to Leave Thee"
Handel, G. F.	"Thanks Be to Thee"
Handel, G. F.	"Wedding Hymn" *(Ptolemy)*
Hopson, Hal	"The Gift of Love"
Jackson, Borghild/Tallois/Busarow	"The Lamps That Light This Wedding Day"
Lovelace, Austin	"A Wedding Benediction"
Pelz, Walter	"A Wedding Blessing"
Proulx, Richard	"Nuptial Blessing"
Vajda, Jarolav/D. Busarow	"Come, Lord Jesus, to This Place"
Wren, Grien/H. Hopson	"Wedding Song"

In addition, the following might be used:

- "O Perfect Love," the hymn by Barnby or by Leo Sowerby

*An inclusive title might be used — "Jesu, Joy of Our Desiring."

- "The Lord Is My Shepherd" (Psalm 23), arranged by many composers
- "Seal Us, O Holy Spirit," the hymn by Meredith

See also Dvorak, *Biblical Songs, Book I* (published by Association Music), for such selections as the following:
- "God Is My Shepherd"
- "I Will Sing New Songs of Gladness"
- "Sing Ye a Joyful Song"

Suggested Hymns for Congregational Use

Processional, Recessional, or in the Service

Hymn	*Tune*
"A Man and Woman We Were Made"	Sussex Carol
"Your Love, O God, Has Called Us Here"	Cornish LM
"O God, You Gave Humanity Its Name"	Sursum Corda
"The Grace of Life Is Theirs"	Rhosymedre
"Jesus, Thou Joy of Loving Hearts"	Rimington
"Joyful, Joyful We Adore Thee"	Hyfrydol
"Now Thank We All Our God"	Nun Danket
"O Perfect Love"	O Perfect Love
"Praise, My Soul, the King of Heaven"	Lauda Anima
"Praise to the Lord, the Almighty"	Lobe Den Herren
"The King of Love My Shepherd Is"	Dominus Regit Me

For Use as a Benediction

"May the Grace of Christ Our Savior"	Sardis

6

GUIDELINES FOR WEDDINGS AND RECEPTIONS

A church without a published official policy statement regarding weddings and receptions would do well to consider drawing one up. Such a statement can prevent misunderstandings and embarrassment when unusual requests are made. And it may relieve the minister, organist, or other individuals of the responsibility for making decisions forced on them by a crisis. It can be either mimeographed or printed in a booklet, and a copy should be given to each bride and groom. Copies should also be available in the church library, office, and vestibule. A sample policy statement will be found in the appendix following this chapter.

The pastor is looked to for leadership in the development of policies regarding weddings, since the wedding service is under his or her sole direction. Usually it is the expressed concern of the pastor which initiates a study of wedding procedures by the church's worship committee or commission. The pastor and organist should serve as advisory members of such a study committee. The committee should study the present practices of the church, policy statements of other churches, and other materials concerned with weddings and receptions in the church.

The committee should submit its complete study to the

governing body of the church for consideration and adoption. Such a report should be as detailed as the particular needs of the local congregation require. It should reflect the church's view of Christian marriage and a business approach to the use of its personnel and facilities for weddings and receptions.

One church located near a large university found it helpful to require a written reservation request for the use of the church's facilities. A deposit, the amount of which is to be determined by the church administrator, is required at the time the reservation is made. In small churches the request is usually made through the church secretary and no deposit is required. The governing bodies of some churches regularly grant permission for the use of church facilities for weddings and receptions.

Some churches charge a fee for the use of their facilities when neither bride nor groom nor their parents are members of the local congregation. Others charge both members and nonmembers a fee to pay for the additional custodial service required at weddings and receptions.

The custodian and other church employees should be paid for the additional work required. The policy statement should indicate either a set amount or an hourly wage for sexton, maid, church hostess, and any other employees.

The job description should indicate whether the church organist is expected to play for rehearsals and weddings as part of his or her duties or whether he or she can expect to receive fees for such services. If the organist is to receive a fee, an amount should be indicated in the policy statement. Some churches stipulate that the church organist is to be paid the usual fee even though the bride may wish to invite a guest organist to play for the wedding.

When professional florists, caterers, and photographers who are not familiar with the church's customs are employed, it is helpful, and sometimes necessary, to furnish them with a list of regulations regarding their services. Such a list should indicate the precautions to be used in decorating the church, the use of candles, the prompt removal of decorations, and the cleaning expected.

Picture Taking and the Reception

In the interview with the bride and groom to discuss the wedding ceremony, the minister should offer suggestions for ways in which pictures can be taken without neglecting the guests who have been invited to the reception. While current practice in many areas calls for immediate picture taking after the ceremony, with guests waiting twenty minutes or half an hour for the reception to begin, this is being altered. The joy of the wedding celebration is not dissipated if the bride and groom, when the reception is held at the church, go immediately to cut the cake and begin the reception. After pictures of the cake cutting are taken, the bridal party returns to the sanctuary for pictures, then goes back to the reception to receive guests formally in a receiving line or to greet them informally. In some churches the bride and groom receive guests in the vestibule as guests leave the sanctuary. The wedding party goes to the reception and then returns to the sanctuary for pictures later. Or pictures may be posed early, before guests arrive.

It is standard practice to prohibit flash pictures until the bride and groom have proceeded to the rear of the church. Even photos taken without a flash can be distracting. The sound of shutters and the aiming of cameras can disturb the dignity and beauty of the ceremony. Some churches require guests to leave their cameras with an usher at the door.

Time exposures by professionals may be permitted if they can be made without disturbing the ceremony or the guests. One church's policy stipulates that photographers are welcome exactly to the extent that they remain inconspicuous. Candid shots usually give a collection of pictures that includes almost everyone. They can be made by an unobtrusive professional or a competent amateur without disrupting the joy of the occasion. The minister should inform photographers of the church's customs to make sure they are familiar with them.

Video or Sound Recording the Ceremony

The minister may suggest that the couple consider having a sound recording or video tape made of the music and ceremony. Some professional services offer this for a fee. Or a good tape recorder that is set for seven inches per second can be used. Some ministers make a tape recording and give it to the couple as a wedding gift, along with a written copy of the service.

Wedding Bulletin

The use of a wedding bulletin is becoming more common. A bulletin announces to the wedding guests that this is a worship service and serves as a memento of the occasion. It also lists the wedding music; members of the wedding party; what participation, if any, is expected of the guests;

and sometimes the couple's new address. Often a brief prayer for the couple is written on the back of the bulletin. Many beautiful and attractive designs are available. They can be either mimeographed or printed. Samples can be had free of charge from the following companies:

Sacred Design Associates
840 Colorado Ave., South
Minneapolis, MN 55416

Conception Abbey Press
Conception, MO 64433

The Liturgical Press
Collegeville, MN 56321

Local church supply stores can also furnish attractive samples.

Honorarium or Fee for the Minister

Honorarium

In most denominations it is customary for the groom to give the minister(s) an honorarium for performing the wedding ceremony. By definition, an honorarium is a payment for professional services for which custom forbids a price to be set. In Roman Catholic churches such gifts belong, by church law, to the parish itself. Professional courtesy dictates that ministers *do not* accept an honorarium when either bride or groom is a member of the ordained clergy. Most of the ministers I interviewed indicate that they *do not* charge a fee for marrying a couple when one or both partners belong to the congregation the minister serves. These ministers indicate that performing weddings is considered part of the work for which they are paid a salary. They may indicate this in a wedding guideline brochure or inform a couple in the first interview.

When an honorarium is given, the minister may choose to use it in a number of creative ways or simply receive it as any other gift. Some ministers return it to the couple on their first anniversary, with a note suggesting that they enjoy an evening out; or the money may be used to buy a book on marriage and family life to give to the couple. Other ministers place it in their discretionary funds. Some refuse the gift, returning it to the groom, but this can seem ungracious on the minister's part.

Fees

When neither bride nor groom is a member of the congregation served by the minister, most clergy charge for their counseling time and for performing the ceremony. This may be negotiable when a couple is on a tight budget or unable to pay. And the minister may choose to waive the fee when couples are prospective members — considered part of the congregation although without formal membership.

An informal survey of one religious group reveals that the average fee runs from $125 to $150. A chaplain in a university ministry of a large state university in the Northeast charges $200 for a wedding. When the wedding is interfaith and the other cleric charges $300 but refuses to conduct the rehearsal, the chaplain charges an equal fee of $300, plus $100 for the rehearsal. I heard of one minister who charged $600 for a wedding. The counseling, rehearsal, and wedding with reception reduce the minister's time to spend with his or her family or in other ways. Most weddings are on Friday or Saturday evening or on Saturday afternoon, the best times for ministers to spend with family or in personal leisure and recreation. When couples spend thousands of dollars on the wedding, the minister, as a professional, should be fairly compensated for the time and energy invested. The minister who charges a fee should explain that it is for the counseling provided as well as for performing the ceremony. A minister who sets a fair fee for weddings will not end up feeling "used" or the victim of an uninformed or thoughtless couple who give no fee or a miserly one.

The minister's honorarium and fee schedule should be discussed and approved by the governing board of the church to avoid misunderstandings. When a minister does charge for weddings, members of the congregation may feel that this is significant income and should compensate for not receiving a raise or an adequate salary. I heard of one church in a town on the border of two states to which many couples came to be married. The church board explained that about half the minister's income was expected to be earned from wedding fees! A minister going to a new church should clarify the church's policy, if any, on wedding fees and on any other fees that might be charged for services rendered, such as counseling.

Alcohol

The church's policy should indicate whether alcohol may be served at receptions in the church. One Episcopal church does not allow alcohol at receptions in the church, so that families may have the option of a church reception without the expense of furnishing champagne for all the guests. The same church's wedding policy states: "It is not in order for any member of the bridal party to come into the church for the wedding or for the rehearsal after having had anything alcoholic to drink." Local customs vary in regard to the use of alcohol, but each church should make known its policy in this regard to prevent embarrassment or misunderstanding.

Smoking

Smoking is generally not allowed in the sanctuary or chapel at any time. Fire regulations and local custom may prohibit it elsewhere, but this should be indicated. Florists should be advised not to smoke in the sanctuary or chapel, where a stray spark on a carpet might cause a fire.

Confetti, Birdseed, and Rice

These are usually not permitted inside the church because of the difficulty involved in cleaning them up. While rice is traditional, and a fertility symbol in some cultures, it should not be used in light of the fact that it can be hazardous to both people and birds. Rice is not only a safety hazard — many people have slipped and fallen on rice, resulting in injury — but it may be dangerous to the birds which eat it, since it expands when moistened. Instead, birdseed may be purchased at hardware stores and pet shops and could be wrapped in individual packets for guests to open and throw at the newlyweds *outside* the church.

The Minister as a Professional

In carrying out her or his role as a professional engaged in marrying couples, the minister has a responsibility to the couple to provide adequate preparation for marriage and follow-up marriage enrichment after the wedding. The minister is paid a salary to do this for members of the congregation served. But for nonmembers an appropriate fee should be charged that includes payment for counseling sessions as well as for conducting the rehearsal and the wedding itself. The fee scale in the following sample wedding policy statement takes this into account. For too long ministers have been willing to be "Marryin' Sams or Suzies" and have failed to do more than hear vows and give the church's blessing. As a professional, the minister should devise a package program (in conjunction with neighboring churches when possible) that includes counseling before and after the wedding and a reasonable fee to compensate for time and skills involved. We do couples a disservice by failing to act as professionals in providing adequate service for which a reasonable fee is charged. Ministers and churches too often are "used" by the general public when weddings are requested.

APPENDIX 2:

SAMPLE POLICY STATEMENT

The Christian Service of Marriage

Introduction

Marriage is a gift God has given to all humankind for the well-being of the entire human family. Marriage is a civil contract between a woman and a man. For Christians marriage is a covenant through which a man and a woman are called to live out together before God their lives of discipleship. In a service of Christian marriage a lifelong commitment is made by a woman and man to each other, publicly witnessed, and acknowledged by the community of faith.

A Service of Worship

Christian marriage should be celebrated in the place where the community gathers for worship. As a service of Christian worship, the marriage service is under the direction of the minister and the supervision of the ses-

---

Reprinted by permission of Rev. Dr. K. C. Ptomey, minister of Westminster Presbyterian Church, Nashville, Tennessee.

sion. The marriage ordinarily takes place in a special service which focuses upon marriage as a gift of God and as an expression of the Christian life.

All weddings held at Westminster Presbyterian Church will be officiated by one of the ordained members of the church staff. Ministers of other denominations may be invited to participate. The invitation must be extended by the church Session.

Ordinarily the wedding service will follow the form found in the *Supplemental Liturgical Resource, 3, Presbyterian Church (USA).* Variations in the elements of the wedding services found in this book may be negotiated with the officiating minister. In every case the order of worship for the wedding will conform to the standards of Reformed Worship as set forth in the Constitution of the Presbyterian Church (U.S.A.).

The service begins with scriptural sentences and a brief statement of purpose. The man and the woman shall declare their intention to enter into Christian marriage and shall exchange vows of love and faithfulness. The service includes appropriate passages of Scripture, which may be interpreted in various forms of proclamation. Prayers shall be offered for the couple, for the communities which support them in this new dimension of discipleship, and for all who seek to live in faithfulness. In the name of the triune God the minister shall declare publicly that the woman and the man are now joined in marriage. A charge may be given. Other actions common to the community and its cultures may appropriately be observed when these actions do not diminish the Christian under-

standing of marriage. The service concludes with a benediction.

Premarital Consultation

In preparation for the marriage service, the minister asked to lead the service shall provide for a discussion with the man and the woman concerning: (1) the nature of their Christian commitment, assuring that at least one is a professing Christian, (2) the legal requirements of the state, (3) the privileges and responsibilities of Christian marriage, (4) the nature and form of the marriage service, (5) the vows and commitments they will be asked to make, (6) the relationships of these commitments to their lives of discipleship, (7) the resources of the faith and the Christian community to assist them in fulfilling their marriage commitments. This discussion is equally important in the case of a first marriage, a marriage after the death of a spouse, and a marriage following divorce.

If the minister is convinced after discussion with the couple that commitment, responsibility, maturity, or Christian understanding are so lacking that the marriage is unwise, the minister shall assure the couple of the church's continuing concern for them and not conduct the ceremony. In making this decision the minister may seek the counsel of the Session.

All persons marrying at Westminster Presbyterian Church will be expected to engage in pre-marital counseling. Appointments for pre-marital counseling should be scheduled well in advance of the wedding. It is the responsibility of the bride and groom to phone the pastor for an appointment.

Wedding Music

Music suitable for the marriage service directs attention to God and expresses the faith of the church. The congregation may join in hymns and other musical forms of praise and prayer.

Before a wedding will be placed on the church calendar the bride and groom will be expected to arrange an appointment with the church musician for the purpose of planning suitable music for the wedding service. One of the organists of the church will play for all weddings. Because a wedding is a worship service, all music must be appropriate to Christian worship. Ordinarily "popular" music, ballads, love songs, etc., are inappropriate in the context of Christian worship. Wedding music, like all music used in worship, should direct our attention to Almighty God and celebrate God's goodness and love. The church musician can offer suitable and appropriate suggestions for all the music of the wedding including processional and recessional music. Ordinarily the Lord's Prayer will not be sung in a wedding service. This is a prayer for the whole people of God and is more appropriately used as a unison prayer voiced by all of those who are in attendance at the service.

The church does not have soloists on staff. However, vocal and/or instrumental solos are a beautiful way to enhance a wedding. It is strongly recommended that when the couple desires solo music, the church musician be involved in the choice of soloists and music. This assures adequate rehearsal of music as well as a high level of artistry for this significant part of your wedding.

In all cases the final decisions regarding the music for a wedding will remain with the church musician in consultation with the pastor. Every effort will be made to provide music which pleases the bride and groom and which is in good taste, as well as in conformity to Presbyterian standards of worship.

Decorations

Flowers, decorations, and other appointments should be appropriate to the place of worship, enhance the worshipers' consciousness of the reality of God, and reflect the integrity and simplicity of Christian life.

The chapel and sanctuary of the church are designed for worship and incorporate symbols of the Christian faith. The two large urns in the Sanctuary have been especially designed to be compatible with the architecture. Ordinarily large flower arrangements in the urns are sufficient decoration for a wedding. Additional decoration is unnecessary. Some families may wish to add candles and perhaps ferns. The church will furnish candelabra which are compatible with Sanctuary decor. The florist should be asked to furnish the candles. If additional decorations are desired, they must not obscure or damage furnishings and symbols in the worship area. Specifically, no arrangements may be placed on or in front of the Communion Table. A floral arrangement may be placed on the retable if it is no taller than the cross. No furniture or symbol will be moved from its usual location in the worship area.

The following precautions will be observed in the decoration of the church:

- The facilities will be available for decorations no more than 4 hours prior to the time of the wedding.
- No nails or screws will be driven into walls, floor, or furnishings.
- Preferably, candles should be used with drip cups, and carpets and other surfaces will be protected from wax drip by a protective cloth.
- Protective cloths or plastic must be placed under all plants containing moisture.
- No candles or arrangements are to be placed on the organ console, pulpit, lectern, baptismal font, or Communion Table. Floral arrangements must not be taller than the cross.
- Aisle cloths (runners) are unnecessary and sometimes unmanageable and therefore will not be allowed.
- No theatrical lights shall be used, nor any other lighting than that which is already part of the sanctuary lighting system.
- All non–church owned decorations will be removed from the facilities immediately following the wedding. The church has no storage areas for such items and will not be responsible for loss or damage.

If families wish to leave wedding flowers for use in worship on the Sunday following the wedding, arrangements should be made through the church office no later than two weeks prior to the wedding. An acknowledgment will be placed in the Sunday bulletin.

Photographs/Videotapes

No photographs will be permitted during a wedding. A picture of the bride and groom leaving the church may be made (with flash if desired) if the photographer does not enter the sanctuary. This picture may be made from the narthex through the double center doors. If the wedding party desires pictures in the chancel area, these may be staged either prior to or following the service.

Videotape machines may be used to record the service if the following guidelines are observed:

1. The equipment shall be placed in the balcony.
2. The equipment shall not obstruct the view of the worshipers sitting in the balcony.
3. *No lights may be used.*

The Rehearsal

The pastor will be responsible for directing the wedding rehearsal. The pastor will be assisted by members of the Wedding Guild. The bride and groom will have filled out a "Rehearsal Information" form prior to the time of the rehearsal. This information will be used by the pastor and members of the Wedding Guild in directing an orderly and expedient rehearsal. If all members of the wedding party are punctual, a rehearsal will take no longer than 45 minutes.

Members of the wedding party are expected to be present at the time set for the rehearsal. Since the rehearsal cannot proceed without all members of the party, latecomers cause the entire party inconvenience and delay the other events of the evening. The pastor will remain 30 minutes after the appointed time for the rehearsal. If all participants have not arrived by that time, the pastor will depart, and the rehearsal will be canceled.

Wedding Guild

The Wedding Guild is a voluntary organization which assists the pastors of the church in directing the wedding rehearsal and in conducting the wedding. A representative of the Guild will contact each bride prior to the wedding and arrange an appointment. The Guild representative will explain wedding procedures at Westminster, answer questions, and in other ways help the family to prepare for the wedding. On the night of the rehearsal members of the Guild will be present to instruct ushers, place members of the wedding party and assure that they get in and out of the church at the appropriate time, and in other ways assist the wedding party. On the wedding day members of the Guild will be present prior to the service to assist the bridesmaids in dressing, to help with any unforeseen difficulties, and to get the members of the wedding party into the church in proper order and on time.

Since the members of the Wedding Guild have done many weddings at Westminster and are familiar with all aspects of church policy and procedure, it becomes unnecessary for the family to hire a wedding director. Members of the Wedding Guild provide their services without charge as a service to their church.

Reception

Both the Fellowship Hall and the parlor areas are available for receptions following weddings at Westminster.

Arrangements for the reception, if held at the church, are to be made in consultation with the church hostess, who will be present to assist the caterer and oversee the use of the kitchen and other church facilities used for the reception. The hostess may be contacted through the church office.

The parlor area can accommodate approximately 150-200 persons, and the Fellowship Hall approximately 350-400.

As a matter of policy, no alcoholic beverages are allowed at wedding receptions held in church facilities.

Receptions at Westminster "move" more freely if guests go directly into the parlor area or the Fellowship Hall following the service (rather than wait outside while the wedding party has pictures taken). If a receiving line or a bride's book are used, they should be placed so as *not* to cause a backlog of persons waiting to enter.

Facilities

In order to rule out possibility of conflict of dates, the sanctuary or chapel may be reserved for particular dates only after staff consultation. A tentative clearance may be given by phone, *but a final reservation can be con-*

firmed only when Form A is returned to the church administrator and the date is entered on the church's Master Calendar.

Weddings may *not* be scheduled for the following days:

- Sundays
- Friday or Saturday prior to Christmas
- Christmas Eve
- Christmas Day
- During Lent (40 days prior to Easter)

Reservations for weddings are scheduled on a "first-come, first-serve" basis for members of Westminster Presbyterian Church.

The church is available on a limited basis to nonmembers for weddings. Reservations cannot be confirmed for nonmembers more than *forty-five* days prior to the date of the wedding. No confirmed date will be given to nonmembers until there has been a consultation with the organist and Form A and a deposit of $25 have been returned to the church administrator. The deposit is nonrefundable after confirmation is given for the wedding date.

The chapel seats approximately 150 persons; the sanctuary approximately 600.

As a matter of policy, no rice, flower petals, or confetti may be thrown by members of the wedding party, either in the church buildings or on the church grounds.

Costs

Fees shall be paid at least seven days prior to the wedding.

Members of the Church

Use of Chapel or Sanctuary	No Charge
Use of Parlor or Fellowship Hall (reception)	No Charge
Pastor (counseling, rehearsal, wedding)	No Charge*
Organist (consultation, rehearsal, wedding)	200.00
Soloist (Vocal soloists or instrumentalists may be engaged. The Organist will assist in finding appropriate musicians.)	Variable
Sexton — Chapel (rehearsal and wedding)	75.00
Sexton — Sanctuary (rehearsal and wedding)	100.00
Sexton — Parlor (reception)	50.00
Sexton — Fellowship Hall (reception)	75.00

*Weddings are a part of the normal responsibility of the pastor and no fee is charged to members for the pastor's service. However, weddings involve additional duties, including pre-marital counseling and the wedding rehearsal as well as the wedding itself. Most families offer an honorarium to the minister. The nonmember fee for the pastor may be used as a guideline for the honorarium.

Nonmembers

Use of Chapel	75.00
Use of Sanctuary	100.00
Use of Parlor or Fellowship Hall (reception)	75.00
Pastor (counseling, rehearsal, wedding)	200.00
Organist (consultation, rehearsal, wedding)	200.00
Soloist (Vocal soloists or instrumentalists may be engaged. The Organist will assist in finding appropriate musicians.)	Variable
Sexton — Chapel (rehearsal and wedding)	75.00
Sexton — Sanctuary (rehearsal and wedding)	100.00

Sexton — Parlor (reception)	50.00
Sexton — Fellowship Hall (reception)	75.00

Hostess

The cost for catering service is negotiated by the parties involved. When outside caterers are employed, the *caterer* will be charged a fee if church dishes are used. The caterer is responsible for clean-up of kitchen facilities and dishes.

The church hostess is required to be present for supervisory purposes when outside caterers are used. This fee is $35.00 and is to be paid by the parties involved. This fee does not include any food preparation or clean-up of facilities.

Rehearsal Information

Entrance of Wedding Party

The wedding party may take their places in a number of different ways. For instance:

a. Groomsmen enter from side of chancel, bridesmaids come down center aisle.
b. Groomsmen enter down center aisle, followed by bridesmaids.
c. Bridesmaids enter down center aisle, on arm of groomsmen.

Bridesmaids and/or groomsmen may enter by center aisle, either singly or in pairs.

Order of Entrance

1. ______________________ ______________________
(If entrance in pairs)
2. ______________________ ______________________
3. ______________________ ______________________
4. ______________________ ______________________
5. ______________________ ______________________
6. ______________________ ______________________
7. ______________________ ______________________
8. ______________________ ______________________
9. ______________________ ______________________
10. ______________________ ______________________
11. ______________________ ______________________
12. ______________________ ______________________

Family to be Seated Separately:

Grandmother of Groom:
1. ____________________ Usher: ____________________
2. ____________________ Usher: ____________________

Grandmother of Bride:
1. ____________________ Usher: ____________________
2. ____________________ Usher: ____________________

Other: ________________ Usher: ____________________

Mother of
Groom: ____________ Usher: ____________________

Mother of
Bride: ______________ Usher: ____________________

Wedding Information

This form must be returned to the Church Administrator before a date is officially confirmed to you by the administrator. Nonmembers must also have a consultation with the organist before a date is officially confirmed.

Bride's Name ________________________________
Address ____________________________________
City, State __________________________________
Zip _______________________________________
Home Phone _________________________________
Work Phone _________________________________
Church Membership ____________________________
Groom's Name _______________________________
Address ____________________________________
City, State __________________________________
Zip _______________________________________
Home Phone _________________________________
Work Phone _________________________________
Church Membership ____________________________
Date of Wedding ______________________________
Day of Week _________________________________
Time ______________________________________
Date of Rehearsal _____________________________

Day of Week ______________________________
Time ______________________________

Place of Wedding [ ] Sanctuary [ ] Chapel
Other ______________________________

It will be: [ ] with floral decorations
[ ] without decorations

Minister: ______________________________

(If you desire a minister from another church to participate in the service, please fill in the following.)

Visiting Minister ______________________________
[ ] Officiate [ ] Assist
Address ______________________________
City, State ______________________________
Zip ______________________________
Church ______________________________
Phone ______________________________

Photographer ______________________________
Address ______________________________
Phone ______________________________

Florist ______________________________
Address ______________________________
Phone ______________________________
Florist will remove decorations when? ____________
Any special use of flowers after wedding? ____________
____

(If you desire someone other than the Church Hostess to cater the wedding, please fill out completely.)

Caterer ____
Address ____
Phone ____

Will there be any social gatherings in the church buildings? [ ] yes [ ] no

[ ] Rehearsal Party in:
  [ ] Parlor Area [ ] Fellowship Hall [ ] Other

[ ] Reception in:
  [ ] Parlor Area [ ] Fellowship Hall [ ] Other

Please designate if other: __________________________

I have read the church's wedding policy and fee schedule. I clearly understand and accept the schedule of charges as outlined.

Please sign _______________________________________
Date ____

For Office Use Only
Date information received: ____________________
Date confirmed: ______________________________
Date fees paid: ______________________________
Organist ____________________________________
Sexton ______________________________________
Minister _____________________________________
Bldg. Use ____________________________________
Other _______________________________________
TOTAL _______________________________________

PART II

MODEL SERVICES

7

A CLASSICAL SERVICE

The Order for the Service of Marriage

The minister is enjoined diligently to instruct those requesting his offices for their prospective marriage in the Christian significance of the holy estate into which they seek to enter.

All arrangements pertaining to the service of marriage shall be made in full consultation with the minister.

This service may begin with a prelude, anthem, solo, or hymn. It may include a processional and recessional and be concluded with a postlude.

The congregation shall stand as the wedding procession begins.

The Christian names of the bride and bridegroom may be used in place of "this man and this woman" in the first, third, and fourth paragraphs.

When the Sacrament of the Lord's Supper is requested, this service should be provided at a time other than the service of marriage.

At the time appointed, the persons to be married, having been qualified according to the laws of the state and the standards of the Church, standing together facing the minister, the man at the minister's left hand and the woman at the right hand, the minister shall say,

Dearly beloved, we are gathered together here in the sight of God, and in the presence of these witnesses, to join together *this man and this woman* in holy matrimony; which is an honorable estate, instituted of God, and signifying unto us the mystical union which exists between Christ and his Church; which holy estate Christ adorned and beautified with his presence in Cana of Galilee. It is therefore not to be entered into unadvisedly, but reverently, discreetly, and in the fear of God. Into this holy estate these two persons come now to be joined. If any man can show just cause why they may not lawfully be joined together, let him now speak, or else hereafter forever hold his peace.

Addressing the persons to be married, the minister shall say,

I require and charge you both, as you stand in the presence of God, before whom the secrets of all hearts are disclosed, that, having duly considered the holy covenant you are about to make, you do now declare before this company your pledge of faith, each to the other. Be well assured that if these solemn vows are kept inviolate, as God's Word demands, and if steadfastly you endeavor to do the will of your heavenly Father, God will bless your marriage, will grant you fulfillment in it, and will establish your home in peace.

Then shall the minister say to the man, using his Christian name,

N., wilt thou have this woman to be thy wedded wife, to live together in the holy estate of matrimony? Wilt thou love her, comfort her, honor and keep her, in sickness and in health; and forsaking all other keep thee only unto her so long as ye both shall live?

The man shall answer,

I will.

Then shall the minister say to the woman, using her Christian name,

N., wilt thou have this man to be thy wedded husband, to live together in the holy estate of matrimony? Wilt thou love him, comfort him, honor and keep him, in sickness and in health; and forsaking all other keep thee only unto him so long as ye both shall live?

The woman shall answer,

I will.

Then shall the minister say,

Who giveth this woman to be married to this man?

The father of the woman, or whoever gives her in marriage, shall answer,

I do.

Then, the minister, receiving the hand of the woman from her father or other sponsor, shall cause the man with his right hand to take the woman by her right hand, and say after him,

I, *N.*, take thee, *N.*, to be my wedded wife, to have and to hold, from this day forward, for better, for worse, for richer, for poorer, in sickness and in health, to love and to cherish, till death us do part, according to God's holy ordinance; and thereto I pledge thee my faith.

Then shall they loose their hands; and the woman, with her right hand taking the man by his right hand, shall say after the minister,

I, *N.*, take thee, *N.*, to be my wedded husband, to have and to hold, from this day forward, for better, for worse, for richer, for poorer, in sickness and in health, to love and to cherish, till death us do part, according to God's holy ordinance; and thereto I pledge thee my faith.

Then they may give to each other rings, or the man may give to the woman a ring, in this wise: the minister, taking the ring or rings, shall say,

The wedding ring is the outward and visible sign of an inward and spiritual grace, signifying to all the uniting of this man and woman in holy matrimony, through the Church of Jesus Christ our Lord.

Then the minister may say,

Let us pray.
Bless, O Lord, the giving of these rings, that they who wear them may abide in thy peace, and continue in thy favor; through Jesus Christ our Lord. **Amen.**

Or, if there be but one ring, the minister may say,

Bless, O Lord, the giving of this ring, that he who gives it and she who wears it may abide forever in thy peace, and continue in thy favor; through Jesus Christ our Lord. **Amen.**

The minister shall then deliver the proper ring to the man to put upon the third finger of the woman's left hand. The man, holding the ring there, shall say after the minister,

In token and pledge of our constant faith and abiding love, with this ring I thee wed, in the name of the Father, and of the Son, and of the Holy Spirit. **Amen.**

Then, if there is a second ring, the minister shall deliver it to the woman to put upon the third finger of the man's left hand; and the woman, holding the ring there, shall say after the minister,

In token and pledge of our constant faith and abiding love, with this ring I thee wed, in the name of the Father, and of the Son, and of the Holy Spirit. **Amen.**

Then shall the minister join their right hands together and, with his hand on their united hands, shall say,

Forasmuch as *N.* and *N.* have consented together in holy wedlock, and have witnessed the same before God and this company, and thereto have pledged their faith each to the other, and have declared the same by joining hands and by giving and receiving *rings;* I pronounce that they are husband and wife together, in the name of the Father, and of the Son, and of the Holy Spirit. Those whom God hath joined together, let not man put asunder. **Amen.**

Then shall the minister say,

Let us pray.

Then shall the husband and wife kneel; the minister shall say,

O eternal God, creator and preserver of all mankind, giver of all spiritual grace, the author of everlasting life: Send thy blessing upon this man and this women, whom we bless in thy name; that they may surely perform and keep the vow and covenant between them made, and may ever remain in perfect love and peace together, and live according to thy laws.

Look graciously upon them, that they may love, honor, and cherish each other, and so live together in faithfulness and patience, in wisdom and true godliness, that their home may be a haven of blessing and a place of peace: through Jesus Christ our Lord. **Amen.**

Then the husband and wife, still kneeling, shall join with the minister and congregation in the Lord's Prayer, saying,

Our Father, who art in heaven, hallowed be thy name. Thy kingdom come, thy will be done on earth as it is in heaven. Give us this day our daily bread. And forgive us our trespasses, as we forgive those who trespass against us. And lead us not into temptation, but deliver us from evil. For thine is the kingdom, and the power, and the glory, forever. Amen.

Then the minister shall give this blessing,

God the Father, the Son, and the Holy Spirit bless, preserve, and keep you; the Lord graciously with his favor look upon you, and so fill you with all spiritual benediction and love that you may so live together in this life that in the world to come you may have life everlasting. **Amen.**

8

A BAPTIST SERVICE

Organ Recital

"Like a Shepherd God Doth Guide Us"	Bach
"Now Thank We All Our God"	Kaufman
Air from Suite for Strings No. 3 in D Major	Bach-Phillips
"Praise to the Lord, the Almighty"	Drischner
"Jesu, Joy of Man's Desiring"	Bach-Grace
The Doxology	Genevan Psalter

Processional

"A Mighty Fortress Is Our God"	Luther-Pachelbel

The Call to Worship

"How beautiful upon the mountains are the feet of him that brings good tidings, that publishes peace." The people everywhere and in all ages have been drawn together in times of tribulation and likewise in times of joy. Thus we

---

This service used by permission of Rev. and Mrs. Deryl Ray Fleming and Dr. Wayne E. Oates, Professor of Psychology and Religion, Southern Baptist Theological Seminary, Louisville, Ken-

have from far places been drawn together this day to witness and to commemorate with a man and a woman their union for the founding among us of a new home. There is in this sacred hour a reverence which moves us to a spirit of worship.

Hymn

"Praise to the Lord, the Almighty"

The Invocation

O Lord, open thou our lips, and our mouth shall show forth thy praise; open thou our minds that we may be enlightened by the truth of thy gospel; open thou our hearts that we may receive the fullness of thy grace; through Jesus Christ our Lord. Amen.

Responsive Reading Psalm 67

May God be gracious to us and bless us and make his face to shine upon us,
That thy ways may be known upon earth, thy saving power among all nations.
Let the people praise thee, O God; let all the people praise thee!
Let the nations be glad and sing for joy, for thou dost judge the peoples with equity and guide the nations upon earth.
Let the peoples praise thee, O God, let all the peoples praise thee!
The earth has yielded its increase; God, our God, has blessed us.
God has blessed us; let all the ends of the earth fear him!

Glory be to the Father, and to the Son, and to the Holy Ghost; as it was in the beginning, is now, and ever shall be, world without end. Amen.

Minister: Let us pray together the prayer our Lord taught us to pray, saying . . .

Our Father which art in heaven, Hallowed be thy name. Thy kingdom come. Thy will be done in earth as it is in heaven. Give us this day our daily bread. And forgive us our trespasses as we forgive those who trespass against us. And lead us not into temptation, but deliver us from evil: For thine is the kingdom, and the power, and the glory, for ever. Amen.

The Scripture

Minister: Hear the reading of the Word of God as it is found in the Moffatt translation of I Corinthians 13:4-8, 13:

Love is very patient, very kind. Love knows no jealousy; love makes no parade, gives itself no airs, is never rude, never selfish, never irritated, never resentful; love is never glad when others go wrong, love is gladdened by goodness, always slow to expose, always eager to believe the best, always hopeful, always patient. Love never disappears. Thus faith and hope and love last on, these three, but the greatest of all is love.

Organist and Choir "O Lord, Most Holy"
Franck

The Service of Holy Matrimony

Minister: Dearly beloved, we are gathered together here in the presence of God and in the fellowship of this Christian community to join together this man and this woman in Christian marriage. Christian marriage is a covenant of faith and trust between a man and a woman, established within their shared commitment in the covenant of faith in Jesus Christ as Lord. Therefore, it requires of both man and woman openness of life and thought, freedom from doubt and suspicion, and commitment to speak the truth in love as they grow up into Christ, who is the head of the Church. Christian marriage, furthermore, is a covenant of hope that endures all things in which both husband and wife commit themselves to interpret each other's behavior with understanding and compassion, and never give up trying to communicate with each other. Christian marriage, therefore, is a covenant of love in which both husband and wife empty themselves of their own concerns and take upon themselves the concerns of each other in loving each other as Christ loved the Church and gave himself for it. Therefore, this covenant is not to be entered into unadvisedly or lightly, but reverently, discreetly, advisedly, and soberly in the fear of God. Into this holy state these two persons come now to be joined.

(Groom), will you have *(Bride)* to be your wedded wife, to live together in the covenant of faith, hope, and love according to the intention of God for your lives together in Jesus Christ? Will you listen to her inmost thoughts, be considerate and tender in your care of her, and stand by her faithfully in sickness and in health, and, preferring her above all others, accept full responsibility for her every necessity as long as you both shall live?

(Bride), will you have *(Groom)* to be your wedded husband, to live together in the covenant of faith, hope, and love according to the intention of God for your lives

together in Jesus Christ? Will you listen to his inmost thoughts, be considerate and helpful in your support of him, and stand by him faithfully in sickness and in health, and, preferring him above all others, accept full responsibility for his every necessity as long as you both shall live?

Minister: Who presents (gives) this woman (these persons) to be married?

Father of Bride: Her mother and I do (or "I do").
or
Parents of Bride and Groom: We do.

(Party moves to platform)

Minister: (Groom) and *(Bride),* will you now express your vows to each other?

The Vows

I, *(Bride/Groom),* take you, *(Groom/Bride),* to be my wedded husband/wife, to have and to hold from this day forward, for better, for worse, for richer, for poorer, in sickness and in health, to love and to understand, till death shall part us, according to the design of God in creation, and commit myself completely to you.

The Ring Ceremony

With this ring I thee wed in the name of the Father and the Son and the Holy Spirit.

The Prayer of Dedication

Minister: Eternal God, make us instruments of thy peace; where hate rules, let us bring love; where malice, forgiveness; where disputes, reconciliation; where error, truth; where doubt, belief; where sorrow, joy. O Lord, let us strive more to comfort others than to be comforted; to understand others more than to be understood; to love others more than to be loved! For he who gives, receives; he who forgets himself, finds; he who forgives, receives forgiveness; and dying we arise again to eternal life through Jesus Christ our Lord. Amen.

The Pronunciation

For as much as *(Groom)* and *(Bride)* have consented together in holy wedlock, and have witnessed the same before God and in the fellowship of this Christian community, and have committed themselves completely to each other, and have declared this by the giving and receiving of the rings, I pronounce that they are husband and wife in the name of the Father and the Son and the Holy Spirit. Amen.

Choral Benediction

"The Lord Bless Thee and Keep Thee" Lutkin

Recessional

Toccata, Symphony 5 Widor

9

AN EPISCOPAL SERVICE

The Celebration and Blessing of a Marriage

Concerning the Service

Christian marriage is a solemn and public covenant between a man and a woman in the presence of God. In The Episcopal Church it is required that one, at least, of the parties must be a baptized Christian; that the ceremony be attested by at least two witnesses; and that the marriage conform to the laws of the State and the canons of this Church.

A priest or a bishop normally presides at the Celebration and Blessing of a Marriage, because such ministers alone have the function of pronouncing the nuptial blessing, and of celebrating the Holy Eucharist.

When both a bishop and a priest are present and officiating, the bishop should pronounce the blessing and preside at the Eucharist.

A deacon, or an assisting priest, may deliver the charge, ask for the Declaration of Consent, read the Gospel, and perform other assisting functions at the Eucharist.

tucky.

Where it is permitted by civil law that deacons may perform marriages, and no priest or bishop is available, a deacon may use the service which follows, omitting the nuptial blessing which follows The Prayers.

It is desirable that the Lessons from the Old Testament and the Epistles be read by lay persons.

In the opening exhortation (at the symbol of *N.N.*), the full names of the persons to be married are declared. Subsequently, only their Christian names are used.

At the time appointed, the persons to be married, with their witnesses, assemble in the church or some other appropriate place.

During their entrance, a hymn, psalm, or anthem may be sung, or instrumental music may be played.

Then the Celebrant, facing the people and the persons to be married, with the woman to the right and the man to the left, addresses the congregation and says

Dearly beloved: We have come together in the presence of God to witness and bless the joining together of this man and this woman in Holy Matrimony. The bond and covenant of marriage was established by God in creation, and our Lord Jesus Christ adorned this manner of life by his presence and first miracle at a wedding in Cana of Galilee. It signifies to us the mystery of the union between Christ and his Church, and Holy Scripture commends it to be honored among all people.

The union of husband and wife in heart, body, and mind is intended by God for their mutual joy; for the help and comfort given one another in prosperity and adversity; and, when it is God's will, for the procreation of children and their nurture in the knowledge and love of the Lord. Therefore marriage is not to be entered into unadvisedly or lightly, but reverently, deliberately, and in accordance with the purposes for which it was instituted by God.

Into this holy union *N.N.* and *N.N.* now come to be joined. If any of you can show just cause why they may not lawfully be married, speak now; or else for ever hold your peace.

Then the Celebrant says to the persons to be married

I require and charge you both, here in the presence of God, that if either of you know any reason why you may not be united in marriage lawfully, and in accordance with God's Word, you do now confess it.

The Declaration of Consent

The Celebrant says to the woman

N., will you have this man to be your husband; to live together in the covenant of marriage? Will you love him, comfort him, honor and keep him, in sickness and in health; and, forsaking all others, be faithful to him as long as you both shall live?

The Woman answers

I will.

The Celebrant says to the man

N., will you have this woman to be your wife; to live together in the covenant of marriage? Will you love her, comfort her, honor and keep her, in sickness and in health;

and, forsaking all others, be faithful to her as long as you both shall live?

The Man answers

I will.

The Celebrant then addresses the congregation, saying

Will all of you witnessing these promises do all in your power to uphold these two persons in their marriage?

We will.

If there is to be a presentation or a giving in marriage, it takes place at this time.

A hymn, psalm, or anthem may follow.

The Ministry of the Word

The Celebrant then says to the people

The Lord be with you.
And also with you.

Let us pray.

O gracious and everliving God, you have created us male and female in your image: Look mercifully upon this man and this woman who come to you seeking your blessing, and assist them with your grace, that with true fidelity and steadfast love they may honor and keep the promises and vows they make; through Jesus Christ our Savior, who lives and reigns with you in the unity of the Holy Spirit, one God, for ever and ever. **Amen.**

Then one or more passages from Holy Scripture is read. If there is to be Communion, a passage from the Gospel always concludes the Readings. A homily or other responses to the Readings may follow.

The Marriage

The Man, facing the woman and taking her right hand in his, says

In the Name of God, I, *N.*, take you, *N.*, to be my wife, to have and to hold from this day forward, for better for worse, for richer for poorer, in sickness and in health, to love and to cherish, until we are parted by death. This is my solemn vow.

Then they loose their hands, and the Woman, still facing the man, takes his right hand in hers, and says

In the Name of God, I, *N.*, take you, *N.*, to be my husband, to have and to hold from this day forward, for better for worse, for richer for poorer, in sickness and in health, to love and to cherish, until we are parted by death. This is my solemn vow.

They loose their hands.

The Priest may ask God's blessing on a ring or rings as follows

Bless, O Lord, *this ring* to be *a sign* of the vows by which this man and this woman have bound themselves to each other; through Jesus Christ our Lord. *Amen.*

The giver places the ring on the ring-finger of the other's hand and says

N., I give you this ring as a symbol of my vow, and with all that I am, and all that I have, I honor you, in the Name of the Father, and of the Son, and of the Holy Spirit (*or* in the Name of God).

Then the Celebrant joins the right hands of husband and wife and says

Now that *N.* and *N.* have given themselves to each other by solemn vows, with the joining of hands and the giving and receiving of *a ring*, I pronounce that they are husband and wife, in the Name of the Father, and of the Son, and of the Holy Spirit.

Those whom God has joined together let no one put asunder.

Amen.

The Prayers

All standing, the Celebrant says

Let us pray together in the words our Savior taught us.

People and Celebrant

Our Father, who art in heaven,
hallowed be thy Name,
thy kingdom come,
thy will be done, on earth as it is in heaven.
Give us this day our daily bread.
And forgive us our trespasses,
as we forgive those who trespass against us.
And lead us not into temptation,

but deliver us from evil.
For thine is the kingdom,
and the power, and the glory,
for ever and ever. Amen.

or

Our Father in heaven,
hallowed be your Name,
your kingdom come,
your will be done, on earth as in heaven.
Give us today our daily bread.
Forgive us our sins
as we forgive those who sin against us.
Save us from the time of trial,
and deliver us from evil.
For the kingdom, the power,
and the glory are yours,
now and for ever. Amen.

If Communion is to follow, the Lord's Prayer may be omitted here.

The Deacon or other person appointed reads the following prayers, to which the People respond, saying, Amen.

If there is not to be a Communion, one or more of the prayers may be omitted.

Let us pray.

Eternal God, creator and preserver of all life, author of salvation, and giver of all grace: Look with favor upon the world you have made, and for which your Son gave his life, and especially upon this man and this woman whom you make one flesh in Holy Matrimony. ***Amen.***

Give them wisdom and devotion in the ordering of their common life, that each may be to the other a strength in need, a counselor in perplexity, a comfort in sorrow, and a companion in joy. ***Amen.***

Grant that their wills may be so knit together in your will, and their spirits in your Spirit, that they may grow in love and peace with you and one another all the days of their life. ***Amen.***

Give them grace, when they hurt each other, to recognize and acknowledge their fault, and to seek each other's forgiveness and yours. ***Amen.***

Make their life together a sign of Christ's love to this sinful and broken world, that unity may overcome estrangement, forgiveness heal guilt, and joy conquer despair. ***Amen.***

Bestow on them, if it is your will, the gift and heritage of children, and the grace to bring them up to know you, to love you, and to serve you. ***Amen.***

Give them such fulfillment of their mutual affection that they may reach out in love and concern for others. ***Amen.***

Grant that all married persons who have witnessed these vows may find their lives strengthened and their loyalties confirmed. ***Amen.***

Grant that the bonds of our common humanity, by which all your children are united one to another, and the living to the dead, may be so transformed by your grace, that your will may be done on earth as it is in heaven; where,

O Father, with your Son and the Holy Spirit, you live and reign in perfect unity, now and for ever. ***Amen.***

The Blessing of the Marriage

The people remain standing. The husband and wife kneel, and the Priest says one of the following prayers

Most gracious God, we give you thanks for your tender love in sending Jesus Christ to come among us, to be born of a human mother, and to make the way of the cross to be the way of life. We thank you, also, for consecrating the union of man and woman in his Name. By the power of your Holy Spirit, pour out the abundance of your blessing upon this man and this woman. Defend them from every enemy. Lead them into all peace. Let their love for each other be a seal upon their hearts, a mantle about their shoulders, and a crown upon their foreheads. Bless them in their work and in their companionship; in their sleeping and in their waking; in their joys and in their sorrows; in their life and in their death. Finally, in your mercy, bring them to that table where your saints feast for ever in your heavenly home; through Jesus Christ our Lord, who with you and the Holy Spirit lives and reigns, one God, for ever and ever. ***Amen.***

or this

O God, you have so consecrated the covenant of marriage that in it is represented the spiritual unity between Christ and his Church: Send therefore your blessing upon these your servants, that they may so love, honor, and cherish each other in faithfulness and patience, in wisdom and true godliness, that their home may be a haven of blessing and peace; through Jesus Christ our Lord, who lives and reigns with you and the Holy Spirit, one God, now and for ever. ***Amen.***

The husband and wife still kneeling, the Priest adds this blessing

God the Father, God the Son, God the Holy Spirit, bless, preserve, and keep you; the Lord mercifully with his favor look upon you, and fill you with all spiritual benediction and grace; that you may faithfully live together in this life, and in the age to come have life everlasting. ***Amen.***

The Peace

The Celebrant may say to the people

The peace of the Lord be always with you.
And also with you.

The newly married couple then greet each other, after which greetings may be exchanged throughout the congregation.

When Communion is not to follow, the wedding party leaves the church. A hymn, psalm, or anthem may be sung, or instrumental music may be played.

10

A LUTHERAN SERVICE

Marriage

Stand

1. The bride, groom, and wedding party stand in front of the minister. The parents may stand behind the couple.

Presiding Minister: The grace of our Lord Jesus Christ, the love of God, and the communion of the Holy Spirit be with you all.

And also with you.

Assisting Minister: Let us pray.
Eternal God, our creator and redeemer, as you gladdened the wedding at Cana in Galilee by your presence of your Son, so by his presence now bring your joy to this wedding. Look in favor upon *N.* and *N.* and grant that they, rejoicing in all your gifts, may at length celebrate with Christ the marriage feast which has no end.
Amen.

Sit

2. *One or more lessons from the Bible may be read. An address may follow. A hymn may be sung.*

A.: The Lord God in his goodness created us male and female, and by the gift of marriage rounded human community in a joy that begins now and is brought to perfection in the life to come.

Because of sin, our age-old rebellion, the gladness of marriage can be overcast and the gift of the family can become a burden.

But because God, who established marriage, continues still to bless it with his abundant and ever-present support, we can be sustained in our weariness and have our joy restored.

P.: N. and *N.*, if it is your intention to share with each other your joys and sorrows and all that the years will bring, with your promises bind yourselves to each other as husband and wife.

Stand

3. *The bride and groom face each other and join hands. Each, in turn, promises faithfulness to the other in these or similar words:*

I take you, *N.*, to be my *wife/husband* from this day forward, to join with you and share all that is to come, and I promise to be faithful to you until death parts us.

4. *The bride and groom exchange rings with these words:*

I give you this ring as a sign of my love and faithfulness.

5. The bride and groom join hands, and the minister announces their marriage by saying:

P.: N. and *N.*, by their promises before God and in the presence of this congregation, have bound themselves to one another as husband and wife.

Blessed be the Father and the Son and the Holy Spirit now and forever.

P.: Those whom God has joined together let no one put asunder.
Amen.

Sit

6. The bride and groom kneel.

P.: The Lord God, who created our first parents and established them in marriage, establish and sustain you, that you may find delight in each other and grow in holy love until your life's end.
Amen.

7. The parents may add their blessing with these or similar words; the wedding party may join them.

May you dwell in God's presence forever; may true and constant love preserve you.

8. The bride and groom stand.

Stand

A.: Let us bless God for all the gifts in which we rejoice today.

P.: Lord God, constant in mercy, great in faithfulness: With high praise we recall your acts of unfailing love for the human family, for the house of Israel, and for your people the Church.

We bless you for the joy which your servants *N.* and *N.* have found in each other, and pray that you give to us such a sense of your constant love that we may employ all our strength in a life of praise of you, whose work alone holds true and endures forever.
Amen.

A.: Let us pray for *N.* and *N.* in their life together.

P.: Faithful Lord, source of love, pour down your grace upon *N.* and *N.*, that they may fulfill the vows they have made this day and reflect your steadfast love in their life-long faithfulness to each other. As members with them of the body of Christ, use us to support their life together; and from your great store of strength give them power and patience, affection and understanding, courage, and love toward you, toward each other, and toward the world, that they may continue together in mutual growth according to your will in Jesus Christ our Lord.
Amen.

Other intercessions may be offered.

A.: Let us pray for all families throughout the world.

P.: Gracious Father, you bless the family and renew your

people. Enrich husbands and wives, parents and children more and more with your grace, that, strengthening and supporting each other, they may serve those in need and be a sign of the fulfillment of your perfect kingdom, where, with your Son Jesus Christ and the Holy Spirit, you live and reign, one God through all ages of ages.
Amen.

9. *When Holy Communion is celebrated, the service continues with the Peace.*

10. *When there is no Communion, the service continues with the Lord's Prayer.*

Our Father in heaven,
hallowed be your Name,
your kingdom come,
your will be done, on earth as in heaven.
Give us today our daily bread.
Forgive us our sins
as we forgive those who sin against us.
Save us from the time of trial,
and deliver us from evil.
For the kingdom, the power,
and the glory are yours,
now and for ever. Amen.

or

Our Father, who art in heaven,
hallowed be thy Name,
thy kingdom come,
thy will be done, on earth as it is in heaven.

Give us this day our daily bread.
And forgive us our trespasses,
as we forgive those who trespass against us;
and lead us not into temptation,
but deliver us from evil.
For thine is the kingdom,
and the power, and the glory,
for ever and ever. Amen.

P.: Almighty God, Father, Son, and Holy Spirit, keep you in his light and truth and love now and forever.
Amen.

11

A PRESBYTERIAN SERVICE

Christian Marriage: Rite I

The following marriage rite is brief and may be used in a variety of settings, although a Christian marriage service should be held in the place where the community of faith gathers for worship.

As a service of Christian worship, the marriage service is under the direction of the minister and the supervision of the session.

Entrance

As the people gather, music appropriate to the praise of God may be offered. At the appointed time the bride, groom, and other members of the wedding party enter and come and stand before the minister. The families of the bride and groom may stand with the couple.

During the entrance of the wedding party, the people may stand and sing a psalm, hymn, or spiritual. Or an anthem may be sung, or instrumental music played.

Sentences of Scripture

The minister calls the people to worship, either before or after the entrance, using one of the following, or another appropriate verse from scripture.

God is love, *1 John 4:16*
and those who abide in love,
abide in God,
and God abides in them.

Statement on the Gift of Marriage

The minister says:

We gather in the presence of God
to give thanks for the gift of marriage,
to witness the joining together of N. and N.,
to surround them with our prayers,
and to ask God's blessing upon them,
so that they may be strengthened for their life together
and nurtured in their love for God.

God created us male and female,
and gave us marriage
so that husband and wife may help and comfort each other,
living faithfully together in plenty and in want,
in joy and in sorrow,
in sickness and in health,
throughout all their days.

God gave us marriage
for the full expression of the love between a man and

a woman.
In marriage a woman and a man belong to each other,
and with affection and tenderness
freely give themselves to each other.

God gave us marriage
for the well-being of human society,
for the ordering of family life,
and for the birth and nurture of children.

God gave us marriage as a holy mystery
in which a man and a woman are joined together,
and become one,
just as Christ is one with the church.

In marriage, husband and wife are called to a new way of life,
created, ordered, and blessed by God.
This way of life must not be entered into carelessly,
or from selfish motives,
but responsibly, and prayerfully.

We rejoice that marriage is given by God,
blessed by our Lord Jesus Christ,
and sustained by the Holy Spirit.
Therefore, let marriage be held in honor by all.

Prayer

The minister says:

Let us pray:
Gracious God,
you are always faithful in your love for us.

Look mercifully upon N. and N.,
who have come seeking your blessing.
Let your Holy Spirit rest upon them
so that with steadfast love
they may honor the promises they make this day,
through Jesus Christ our Savior.
Amen.

The congregation may be seated.

Declarations of Intent

The minister addresses the bride and groom individually, using either A or B:

A

N., understanding that God has created, ordered,
and blessed the covenant of marriage,
do you affirm your desire and intention to enter
this covenant?

Answer:

I do.

B

If both are baptized, the following may be used:

N., in your baptism
you have been called to union with Christ and
the church.
Do you intend to honor this calling
through the covenant of marriage?

Answer:

I do.

The minister may address the families of the bride and groom.

N., N. *[Names of family members],*
do you give your blessing to N. and N.,
and promise to do everything in your power to uphold them in their marriage?

The families of the bride and groom answer:

1

We (I) give our (my) blessing and promise our (my) loving support.

Or

2

We (I) do.

The families of the bride and groom may be seated.

Affirmation of the Congregation

The minister may address the congregation, saying:

Will all of you witnessing these vows do everything in your power to uphold N. and N. in their marriage?

Answer:

We will.

A psalm, hymn, spiritual, or anthem may be sung.

Reading from Scripture

The following, or a similar prayer for illumination, may be said.

God of mercy,
your faithfulness to your covenant
frees us to live together
in the security of your powerful love.

Amid all the changing words of our generation,
speak your eternal Word that does not change.
Then may we respond to your gracious promises
by living in faith and obedience;
through our Lord Jesus Christ.
Amen.

One or more scripture passages are read.

Sermon

After the scriptures are read, a brief sermon may be given. A psalm, hymn, spiritual, or other music may follow.

Vows

The people may stand.

The minister addresses the couple:

N. and N.,
since it is your intention to marry,

join your right hands,
and with your promises
bind yourselves to each other as husband and wife.

The bride and groom face each other and join right hands. They in turn then make their vows to each other, using A or B.

A

The man says:

I, N., take you, N., to be my wife:
and I promise,
before God and these witnesses,
to be your loving and faithful husband;
in plenty and in want;
in joy and in sorrow;
in sickness and in health;
as long as we both shall live.

The woman says:

I, N., take you, N., to be my husband;
and I promise,
before God and these witnesses,
to be your loving and faithful wife;
in plenty and in want;
in joy and in sorrow;
in sickness and in health;
as long as we both shall live.

B

The man says:

Before God and these witnesses,
I, N., take you, N., to be my wife,
and I promise to love you,
and to be faithful to you,
as long as we both shall live.

The woman says:

Before God and these witnesses
I, N., take you, N., to be my husband,
and promise to love you,
and to be faithful to you,
as long as we both shall live.

Exchange of Rings (or Other Symbols)

If rings are to be exchanged, the minister may say to the couple:

What do you bring as the sign of your promise?

When the rings are presented, the minister may say the following prayer.

By your blessing, O God,
may these rings be to N. and N.
symbols of unending love and faithfulness,
reminding them of the covenant they have made
this day,
through Jesus Christ our Lord.
Amen.

The bride and groom exchange rings using A or B or other appropriate words. The traditional trinitarian formula should be omitted for both the bride and groom if one of the marriage partners is not a professing Christian.

A

The one giving the ring says:

N., I give you this ring as a sign of our covenant,
in the name of the Father,
and of the Son,
and of the Holy Spirit.

The one receiving the ring says:

I receive this ring as a sign of our covenant,
in the name of the Father,
and of the Son,
and of the Holy Spirit.

B

As each ring is given, the one giving the ring says:

This ring I give you,
as a sign of our constant faith
and abiding love,
in the name of the Father,
and of the Son,
and of the Holy Spirit.

Prayer

The couple may kneel.

One of the following prayers, or a similar prayer, is said:

Let us pray:

1

Eternal God,
Creator and preserver of all life,
author of salvation, and giver of all grace:
look with favor upon the world you have made and
redeemed,
and especially upon N. and N.

Give them wisdom and devotion
in their common life,
that each may be to the other
a strength in need,
a counselor in perplexity,
a comfort in sorrow,
and a companion in joy.

Grant that their wills
may be so knit together in your will,
and their spirits in your Spirit,
that they may grow in love and peace
with you and each other
all the days of their life.

Give them the grace,
when they hurt each other,
to recognize and confess their fault,
and to seek each other's forgiveness
and yours.

Make their life together

a sign of Christ's love
to this sinful and broken world,
that unity may overcome estrangement,
forgiveness heal guilt,
and joy conquer despair.

Give them such fulfillment of their mutual love
that they may reach out in concern for others.

[Give to them, if it is your will,
the gift of children,
and the wisdom to bring them up
to know you,
to love you,
and to serve you.]

Grant that all who have witnessed these vows today
may find their lives strengthened,
and that all who are married
may depart with their own promises renewed.

Enrich with your grace
all husbands and wives, parents and children,
that, loving and supporting one another,
they may serve those in need
and be a sign of your kingdom.

Grant that the bonds by which all your children
are united to one another
may be so transformed by your Spirit
that your peace and justice may fill the earth,
through Jesus Christ our Lord.
Amen.

2

Eternal God,
without your grace no promise is sure.
Strengthen N. and N.
with patience, kindness, gentleness,
and all other gifts of the Spirit,
so that they may fulfill the vows they have made.
Keep them faithful to each other and to you.
Fill them with such love and joy
that they may build a home of peace and welcome.
Guide them by your Word
to serve you all their days.

Help us all, O God,
to do your will in each of our homes and lives.
Enrich us with your grace
so that, supporting one another,
we may serve those in need
and hasten the coming of peace, love, and justice
on earth,
through Jesus Christ our Lord.
Amen.

The minister invites all present to sing or say the Lord's Prayer.

As our Savior Christ has taught us, we are bold to say:

All pray together.

Our Father in heaven,
hallowed be your name,

Or

Our Father, who art in heaven,

your kingdom come,
your will be done,
on earth as in heaven.
Give us today our
daily bread.
Forgive us our sins
as we forgive those who
sin against us.
Save us from the time
of trial
and deliver us from evil.
For the kingdom, the
power, and the glory
are yours now and
forever. Amen.

hallowed be thy name,
thy kingdom come,
thy will be done,
on earth as it is in heaven.
Give us this day our daily
bread;
and forgive us our debts,
as we forgive our debtors;
and lead us not into
temptation,
but deliver us from evil.
For thine is the kingdom,
and the power, and the
glory, forever. Amen.

Announcement of Marriage

The minister addresses the congregation:

Before God
and in the presence of this congregation,
N. and N. have made their solemn vows to each other.
They have confirmed their promises by the joining
of hands
[and by the giving and receiving of rings].
Therefore, I proclaim that they are now husband
and wife.
Blessed be the Father and the Son and the Holy Spirit
now and forever.

The minister joins the couple's right hands.

The congregation may join the minister saying:

Those whom God has joined together
let no one separate.

Charge to the Couple

The minister addresses the couple, using one of the following:

1 *See Col. 3:12-14*

As God's own,
clothe yourselves with compassion,
kindness, and patience,
forgiving each other
as the Lord has forgiven you,
and crown all these things with love,
which binds everything together in perfect harmony.

2 *Col. 3:17*

Whatever you do, in word or deed,
do everything in the name of the Lord Jesus,
giving thanks to God through him.

Blessing

The minister gives God's blessing to the couple and the congregation, using one of the following:

1 *See Num. 6:24-26*

The Lord bless you and keep you.
The Lord be kind and gracious to you.

The Lord look upon you with favor
and give you peace.
Amen.

2

The grace of Christ attend you,
the love of God surrounding you,
the Holy Spirit keep you,
that you may live in faith,
abound in hope,
and grow in love,
both now and forevermore.
Amen.

A psalm, hymn, spiritual, or anthem may be sung, or instrumental music may be played, as the wedding party leaves.

12

A UNITED METHODIST SERVICE

A Service of Christian Marriage

The Entrance

Gathering

While the people gather, instrumental or vocal music may be offered.

During the entrance of the wedding party, there may be instrumental music or a hymn, a psalm, a canticle, or an anthem.

Greeting

Minister: Friends, we are gathered together in the sight of God to witness and to bless the joining together of *N.* and *N.* in Christian marriage. The covenant of marriage was established by God, who created us male and female for each other. With his presence and power, Jesus graced a wedding at Cana of Galilee and in his

---

sacrificial love gave us the example for the love of husband and wife. *N.* and *N.* come to give themselves to one another in this holy covenant.

Declaration of Intention

Minister to the persons who are to marry:

I ask you now
in the presence of God and these people
to declare your intention
to enter into union with one another
through the grace of Jesus Christ,
who has called you into union with himself
through baptism.

Minister to the woman:

N., will you have *N.* to be your husband,
to live together in holy marriage?
Will you love him, comfort him, honor and keep him
in sickness and in health,
and forsaking all others, be faithful to him
as long as you both shall live?

Woman:

I will.

Minister to the man:

N., will you have *N.* to be your wife,
to live together in holy marriage?
Will you love her, comfort her, honor and keep her
in sickness and in health,

and forsaking all others, be faithful to her
as long as you both shall live?

Man:

I will.

The Response of the Families and People

Minister: The marriage of *N.* and *N.* unites two families
and creates a new one.
They ask for your blessing.

Parents or other representatives of the families, if present, may respond:

**We rejoice in your union,
and pray God's blessing upon you.**

Minister: Will all of you, by God's grace,
do everything in your power
to uphold and care for these two persons
in their marriage?

We will.

Prayer

Minister: The Lord be with you.

And also with you.

Minister:
Let us pray.
God of all peoples:
You are the true light illumining everyone.

You show us the way, the truth, and the life.
You love us even when we are disobedient.
You sustain us with your Holy Spirit.
We rejoice in your life in the midst of our lives.
We praise you for your presence with us,
and especially in this act of solemn covenant.
Through Jesus Christ our Lord.
Amen.

Proclamation and Response

One or more Scripture lessons are read.

A hymn, psalm, canticle, anthem, or other music may be offered before or after readings.

A sermon or other witness to Christian marriage is given.

Extemporaneous intercessory prayer may be offered, or the following may be prayed by the minister or by all:

Let us pray.
Eternal God,
creator and preserver of all life,
author of salvation, giver of all grace:
Bless and sanctify with your Holy Spirit
N. and *N.* who come now to join in marriage.
Grant that they may give their vows to each other
in the strength of your steadfast love.
Enable them to grow in love and peace
with you and with one another all their days,
that they may reach out
in concern and service to the world,
through Jesus Christ our Lord. **Amen.**

The Marriage

Exchange of Vows

The woman and man face each other, joining hands.

Man to woman:

In the name of God,
I, *N.*, take you, *N.*,
to be my wife,
to have and to hold
from this day forward,
for better for worse,
for richer for poorer,
in sickness and in health,
to love and to cherish,
until we are parted by death.
This is my solemn vow.

Woman to man:

In the name of God,
I, *N.*, take you, *N.*,
to be my husband,
to have and to hold
from this day forward,
for better for worse,
for richer for poorer,
in sickness and in health,
to love and to cherish,
until we are parted by death.
This is my solemn vow.

Blessing and Exchange of Rings

The minister may say:

These rings *(symbols)*
are the outward and visible sign
of an inward and spiritual grace,
signifying to us the union
between Jesus Christ and his Church.

The minister may bless the giving of rings or other symbols of the marriage.

Bless, O Lord, the giving of these rings *(symbols)*, that they who wear them may live in your peace, and continue in your favor all the days of their life, through Jesus Christ our Lord. **Amen.**

The giver(s) may say to the recipient(s):

N., I give you this ring (symbol)
as a sign of my vow,
and with all that I am,
and all that I have,
I honor you
in the name of the Father,
and of the Son,
and of the Holy Spirit.

Declaration of Marriage

The wife and husband join hands. The minister may place a hand on, or wrap a stole around, their joined hands.

Minister to husband and wife:

You have declared your consent and vows
before God and this congregation.
May God confirm your covenant
and fill you both with grace.

Minister to people:

Now that *N.* and *N.*
have given themselves to each other by solemn vows,
with the joining of hands,
and the giving and receiving of *rings,*
I announce to you that they are husband and wife
in the name of the Father, and of the Son, and of the Holy Spirit.
Those whom God has joined together,
let no one put asunder.
Amen.

A doxology or other hymn may be sung.

Intercessions may be offered for the Church and for the world.

Blessing of the Marriage

The husband and wife may kneel, as the minister prays:

O God,
you have so consecrated the
covenant of Christian marriage
that in it is represented
the covenant between Christ and his Church.
Send therefore your blessing upon *N.* and *N.*,
that they may surely keep their marriage covenant

and so grow in love and godliness together,
that their home may be a haven
of blessing and peace,
through Jesus Christ our Lord.
Amen.

If Holy Communion is not to be celebrated, the service continues with the Lord's Prayer and concludes with the Sending Forth.

SENDING FORTH

Here a hymn may be sung or Psalm 128 may be read.

Dismissal with Blessing

God the Eternal keep you in love with each other,
so that the peace of Christ may abide in your home.
Go to serve God and your neighbor in all that you do.

Bear witness to the love of God in this world
so that those to whom love is a stranger
will find in you generous friends.
The grace of the Lord Jesus Christ,
and the love of God,
and the communion of the Holy Spirit be with you all.
Amen.

The Peace

The peace of the Lord be with you always.

And also with you.

The couple and minister(s) may greet each other, after which greetings may be exchanged throughout the congregation.

Going Forth

A hymn may be sung or instrumental music played as the couple, the wedding party, and the people leave.

13

THE BLESSING OF A CIVIL MARRIAGE

Before conducting the service the minister should be certain that the couple seeking this blessing have, in fact, been lawfully married. A copy of the signed marriage certificate is desirable.

This service may be conducted during or at the conclusion of a regular worship service, or as a separate service. If conducted during a service, the declaration of intent and other nonessentials may be omitted.

ENTRANCE

The couple present themselves before the minister. This may be done with the traditional processional, or the couple may move from a church pew to a position in front of the minister. The families of the couple may stand with them. Music may be played as they take their places.

WORDS OF SCRIPTURE

The people assembled may be called to worship with the following or similar words from Scripture:

This service was composed by Perry H. Biddle, Jr.

Minister: Give thanks to the Lord, for the Lord is good.

God's love endures forever.

Statement concerning Marriage

Minister: N. and *N.* have been married according to the laws of _____. They have made their commitment to each other in vows recognized by the governing authorities. Now they come to reaffirm those vows and to ask for God's blessing on their marriage. We gather to witness their promises to each other and to affirm their relationship in marriage.

God created marriage and has sanctified marriage. Jesus, by his presence at the marriage of Cana in Galilee, gave his blessing to marriage. In Jesus' sacrificial love he has given us an example for the love of husband and wife. The Scriptures command us to love our neighbor, and in the marriage relationship, our nearest neighbor is our husband or wife. Scripture teaches us to "be kind to one another, tenderhearted, forgiving one another, as God in Christ forgave you" (Eph. 4:32).

Our vows in marriage are acts of our will, by which we pledge our faithfulness to each other for life. We are to love and care for each other in all circumstances of life — in sickness and trouble, in sorrow and distress, as well as in times of joy and wholeness. We are to provide each other and our household with the things that make life possible and add beauty and zest. And we are to pray for and with each other, offering our thanks to God for his love and the love we share in marriage.

There is a mystery about marriage — a man and a

woman are joined together and become one, even as Christ is one with the church. In marriage a wife and husband are called by God to a new way of life, a life of being best friends, accepting each other in spite of differences, a life of expressing care for each other.

Prayer

The minister offers a brief prayer of blessing on the couple, asking God's Holy Spirit to rest upon them so that their vows may be honored.

Declaration of Intent

The minister addresses the man and the woman separately:

N., you have heard the scriptural blessing of Christian marriage. Do you wish to affirm your vow to *N.* in the presence of God and the church?

Answer: I do.

Affirmation of the Families

The minister speaks to the parents and other family members:

Do you give your blessing to *N.* and *N.* and promise to encourage and support them in their Christian marriage?

Answer: (I/we) give (my/our) blessing and promise to encourage and support them in their marriage.

If the families are standing they may be seated.

Affirmation of the Congregation

The minister speaks the following or similar words to the congregation. The congregation may stand if desired.

Will you, the friends of *N.* and *N.*, encourage and affirm them in their Christian marriage?

We will.

A hymn may be sung, or music suitable to the occasion may be played.

Scripture

Wedding Homily

Additional music such as a hymn or instrumental music may be used.

The Vows

Minister: N. and *N.*, join your right hands as you make your solemn vows to each other.

The couple face each other, join right hands and look into each other's eyes (when possible) and say their vows in the following or similar words:

Husband: N., you are my wife, and now I promise before God and this congregation as witnesses that I will be your loving and faithful husband in times of plenty and in want, in joy and in sorrow, in sickness and in health, as long as we both shall live.

Wife: N., you are my husband, and now I promise before God and this congregation as witnesses that I will be your loving and faithful wife in times of plenty and in want, in joy and in sorrow, in sickness and in health, as long as we both shall live.

The couple may kneel. The minister leads a prayer; the congregation then joins in the Lord's Prayer.

The minister joins the couple's right hands and may place the clergy stole on their joined hands.

Minister: Those whom God has joined together let no one separate.

A brief charge of instruction and encouragement is given to the couple in words of Scripture or in the minister's own words.

Benediction

The couple may greet each other with a kiss.
Music may be sung or played as the couple and the wedding party leave.

BIBLIOGRAPHY

Arond and Pauker. *First Year of Marriage.* New York: Warner Books, 1987. Tells newlyweds what to expect in their first year of marriage and how to deal with money, family, decision making, communication, etc.

Barbach, Lonnie. *For Each Other: Sharing Sexual Intimacy.* New York: New American Library, 1984. An outstanding book for couples to read and discuss as they prepare for marriage.

———. *For Yourself: The Fulfillment of Female Sexuality.* New York: Doubleday & Co., 1975. Excellent resource to be read by both men and women preparing for marriage.

Biddle, Perry H., Jr. *Marrying Again.* Nashville: Abingdon Press, 1986. A resource for couples planning a second wedding. Stresses the importance of "realized forgiveness" by and for persons whose previous marriage(s) ended in divorce. Provides guidance for minister and couple in planning the second wedding ceremony.

———. *The Goodness of Marriage.* Nashville: The Upper Room, 1984. Designed as a gift book for newlyweds, this devotional book contains meditations and prayers on the major topics of marriage for the first twenty-eight days (four weeks) of marriage. May be given to the couple during premarital counseling or on the day of the wedding.

Book of Common Worship. Prepared by the Theology and Worship Unit of the Presbyterian Church (U.S.A.). Louisville: Westminster/John Knox Press, 1993. Contains the newest Presbyterian liturgies and worship aids, including several versions of the marriage service.

Burghardt, Walter J., S.J. *Grace on Crutches.* Mahwah, N.J.: Paulist Press, 1986. Some fine wedding homilies are included in this collection of sermons on lectionary texts. Preached in the Georgetown University chapel by a "preacher's preacher."

Carnes, Andrew. *Divorce and Remarriage.* Grand Rapids: Wm. B. Eerdmans Publishing Co., 1993. A balanced combination of biblical perspective and practical, pastoral experience helpful for couples planning a second marriage and for pastors counseling them.

Clinebell, Charlotte Holt. *Meet Me in the Middle: On Being Human Together.* New York: Harper & Row, 1973. Discusses effects of the women's liberation movement on both husband and wife in marriage. A chapter by the author's husband gives his reactions to changes that have occurred in their marriage.

Cultos Principales de la Iglesia. Nashville: Ediciones Discipulado (Disciples Resources). Contains "Un Servico de Matrimonio Christiano," p. 12.

Emerson, James G. *Divorce, the Church and Remarriage.* Philadelphia: Westminster Press, 1961. Although out of print, this book can be found in libraries and is a solid theological study of the subject. Very useful in counseling divorced persons planning a second marriage.

Grace, Mike, and Joyce Grace. *A Joyful Meeting: Sexuality in Marriage.* International Marriage Encounter, Inc., 955 Lake Dr., St. Paul, MN 55120. Published 1984. The authors are a husband/wife team of medical doctors in Winnipeg, Canada, the parents of eight children. The book combines sexuality and spirituality so that they naturally belong together. The authors deal with the real but subtle gender differences.

Hine, James R. *How to Have a Long, Happy, Healthy Marriage.* Danville: Interstate Publishers, 1985. Gives sound, practical advice for couples building a marriage in today's complicated society.

———. *The Springtime of Love and Marriage.* Valley Forge: Judson Press, 1985. Written to guide couples in the early years of marriage. Will help couples nourish their love until it blossoms into a rich, growing marriage relationship.

Hunt, Joan, and Richard Hunt. *Preparing for Christian Marriage.* Nashville: Abingdon Press, 1982. A companion to the Antoinette and Leon Smith book by the same title. This book for couples helps them explore their deepest feelings and thoughts; deals with sex, money, children, work, etc. Living space and household chores are covered in a very helpful way.

Klausner, Abraham, J. *Weddings: A Complete Guide to All Religious and Interfaith Marriage Services.* New York: New American Library, 1988. A useful resource for the minister.

Mace, David R. *Close Companions.* New York: Continuum Publishing Co., 1982. The basic text for understanding marriage enrichment. Defines the new "partnership" marriage or companionship in marriage. A good resource for pastors and couples in developing marriage enrichment programs.

———. *Getting Ready for Marriage: Revised.* Nashville: Abingdon Press, 1985. One of the best books in the field. Can be given to couples to read after their first interview for marriage planning. Deals with the major topics of marriage in a clear and practical fashion.

Mace, David R., and Vera Mace. *How to Have a Happy Marriage.* Nashville: Abingdon Press, 1977. An outstanding book for couples, giving step-by-step guidance to an enriched marriage relationship.

———. *In the Presence of God.* Philadelphia: Westminster Press, 1985. An inspiring collection of readings for newly married couples by two leaders of marriage enrichment programs.

———. *Love and Anger in Marriage.* Winston-Salem: A.C.M.E., 1993. Helps couples learn how to feel and work through anger in a positive way.

———. *When the Honeymoon's Over: Make the Most of Your First Year of Marriage.* Nashville: Abingdon Press, 1988. Excellent resource for use with couples alone or in groups.

Marriage Encounter, Inc., 955 Lake Drive, St. Paul, MN 55120. Offers a wide variety of books and other materials for ministers and couples in preparing for marriage and enriching marriage. Write for free catalogue.

Peck, M. Scott. *The Road Less Traveled.* New York: Simon & Schuster, 1978. A best seller for many years about human relationships. The section on "The Myth of Romantic Love" should be read by all couples preparing for marriage.

Penner, Clifford, and Joyce Penner. *The Gift of Sex.* St. Paul: Marriage Encounter, Inc., 1981. A guide to understanding sex based on research that explores its spiritual aspects.

Pitt, Theodore K. *Premarital Counseling Handbook for Ministers.* Valley Forge: Judson Press, 1985. An excellent resource for the minister in planning a program of premarital counseling. Suggests eight sessions in a workshop approach, with the couple alone or with a group.

Prepare-Enrich, P.O. Box 190, Minneapolis, MN 55440. The "Prepare" materials are for couples preparing for marriage. "Enrich" is for couples already married. Both are excellent tools for the minister to use with couples. Tests are computer scored. Write for sample materials. Highly recommended by ministers and counselors.

The Resource Center, The Association for Couples in Marriage Enrichment (ACME), Box 10596, Winston-Salem, NC 27108; Tel. 1-800-634-8325. Ask for books and resources catalogue. Can furnish resources to use in preparing couples for marriage and guidance in setting up marriage enrichment programs for newlyweds. Founded by Vera Mace and her late husband, David. Highly recommended.

Smith, Antoinette, and Leon Smith. *Preparing for Christian Marriage: Pastor's Manual.* Nashville: Abingdon Press, 1982. The best guide available for the pastor in planning a comprehensive program of premarital counseling. Written by a consultant-trainer couple, this book helps couples understand marriage in light of the Christian faith. Should be used with Joan and Richard Hunt's book by the same title, the couples' guidebook.

The United Methodist Book of Worship. Nashville: The United Methodist Publishing House, 1992. Contains slightly revised versions of the liturgies in *The Book of Services* of 1985. Note: The services of *The Book of Worship* were not available from the publisher for inclusion in this edition.

Wheat, Ed., M.D., and Gaye Wheat. *Intended for Pleasure.* Grand Rapids: Fleming H. Revell, 1993. A revised classic resource on sexual pleasure in marriage written by a Christian physician and his wife.

Zilbergeld, Bernie. *Male Sexuality.* Boston: Little Brown, 1978. Highly recommended reading for both men and women preparing for marriage.

ABOUT THE AUTHOR

PERRY H. BIDDLE, JR., is an author and minister-at-large of Middle Tennessee Presbytery, Presbyterian Church (USA). He is a graduate of Davidson College, Davidson, North Carolina, Union Theological Seminary in Virginia, Richmond, Virginia, and Vanderbilt University, Nashville, Tennessee. He also studied at New College, University of Edinburgh, Scotland. He is the author of fifteen books, including *A Marriage Manual, A Hospital Visitation Manual,* and *A Funeral Manual,* three highly acclaimed books on pastoral care.